HOW CHILDREN AND ADOLESCENTS EVALUATE GENDER AND RACIAL EXCLUSION

Melanie Killen
Jennie Lee-Kim
Heidi McGlothlin
Charles Stangor

WITH COMMENTARY BY
Charles C. Helwig

Willis F. Overton
Series Editor

ETY FOR RESEARCH IN CHILD DEVELOPMENT
Serial No. 271, Vol. 67, No. 4, 2002

 **Blackwell**
Publishing

Boston, Massachusetts   Oxford, United Kingdom

HOW CHILDREN AND ADOLESCENTS EVALUATE GENDER AND RACIAL EXCLUSION

CONTENTS

COMMENTARY

ABSTRACT

KILLEN, MELANIE; LEE-KIM, JENNIE; McGLOTHLIN, HEIDI; and STANGOR, CHARLES. How Children and Adolescents Evaluate Gender and Racial Exclusion. *Monographs of the Society for Research in Child Development*, 2002, **67** (4, Serial No. 271).

Children's and adolescents' social reasoning about exclusion was assessed in three different social contexts. Participants ($N = 294$) at three ages, 10 years (4th grade), 13.7 years (7th grade), and 16.2 years (10th grade), fairly evenly divided by gender, from four ethnic groups, European-American ($n = 109$), African-American ($n = 96$), and a combined sample of Asian-American and Latin-American participants ($n = 89$) were interviewed regarding their social reasoning about exclusion based on group membership, gender, and race. The contexts for exclusion were friendship, peer, and school. Significant patterns of reasoning about exclusion were found for the context, the target (gender or race) of exclusion, and the degree to which social influence, authority expectations, and cultural norms explained children's judgments. There were also significant differences depending on the gender, age, and ethnicity of the participants. The findings support our theoretical proposal that exclusion is a multifaceted phenomenon and that different forms of reasoning are brought to bear on the issue. This model was drawn from social-cognitive domain theory, social psychological theories of stereotype knowledge and intergroup relationships, and developmental studies on peer relationships. The results contribute to an understanding of the factors involved in the developmental emergence of judgments about exclusion based on group membership as well as to the phenomena of prejudice, discrimination, and the fair treatment of others.

I: INTRODUCTION, THEORETICAL BACKGROUND, AND PRIOR RESEARCH

> . . . child morality throws light on adult morality. If we want to form men and women, nothing will fit us so well for the task as to study the laws that govern their formation.
>
> Jean Piaget, *The Moral Judgment of the Child*

> Thought finds a greater difficulty in dealing with our grasp of group events (than with perceiving individuals), despite the fact that we act as members of groups and deal with others in terms of their group membership. A prominent reason for this difficulty is that human groups, unlike things, consist of a multiplicity of individuals or units, each of which is itself a highly complex system.
>
> Solomon Asch, *Social Psychology*

> If we operate with a determinate conception of the human being that is meant to have some normative moral and political force, we must also, in applying it, ask which beings we take to fall under the concept. And . . . all too easily . . . the powerless can be excluded.
>
> Martha Nussbaum, *Sex and Social Justice*

Exclusion from social groups is a source of conflict, stress, and tension in social life around the globe. If we are to address the multitude of problems that we witness around the world among and between groups, cultures, religions, and countries, it is important to understand the developmental origins of exclusion. How does one explain exclusion? What makes it legitimate? When is it wrong, why is it wrong, and how do we conceptualize such acts? At what points in development do children begin to exclude one another on the basis of gender, race, and ethnicity? What do children think about exclusion, and what forms of reasoning do they use in making decisions related to it? As Solomon Asch (1952) has elegantly written, understanding individual social cognition about social groups requires analyzing the complexities of social groups. In so doing we must also define the parameters of the group—that is, who is included

1

and who is excluded. We propose that these types of decisions involve multiple considerations, and addressing these issues involves conducting research that is informed by multidisciplinary lines of research and scholarship.

There is surprisingly little research on how children evaluate exclusion from groups despite the rather large output of work on stereotyping, intergroup relationships, peer rejection, moral reasoning, and cultural norms and conventions. We have drawn from different avenues of research to formulate a research program designed to investigate how children evaluate exclusion from social groups, relationships, and institutions. Our research has emerged over the past five years and reflects only the beginning of a line of work necessary to fully understand this complex phenomenon. The events of the fall of September, 2001, point to the need to better understand how individuals reason about exclusion, when it is a legitimate decision designed to preserve group functioning, and when it is an unfair decision designed to perpetuate discrimination, inequality, and oppression. How do individuals deal with decisions that involve conflicts between group functioning, on the one hand, and unfairness, on the other hand? Most relevant to our inquiry is the developmental question: What are the developmental origins of these types of judgments? How do children and adolescents evaluate exclusion based on group membership and when do stereotypes, biases, and fairness judgments enter into decision-making about exclusion? These questions guided our research program, one that constitutes a very preliminary inquiry into this vexed and complicated aspect of human life.

In developmental psychology, much of the research on exclusion from social groups has focused on peer rejection (Asher & Coie, 1990; Rubin, Bukowski, & Parker, 1998) and, more recently, peer victimization (Graham & Juvonen, 1998). Studies in the area of children's social competence have demonstrated that children who are rejected from social groups experience a wide range of negative consequences that bear on the children's trajectories for healthy social development (Rubin et al., 1998). For example, children who are rejected from social groups are at risk for poor academic achievement, increased depression, and adolescent delinquency (Asher & Coie, 1990; Graham & Juvonen, 1998; Graham & Taylor, 2002; Rubin, Coplan, Nelson, Cheah, & Lagace-Seguin, 1999). This result is further borne out by research on interpersonal rejection in adult interactions, which also finds that interpersonal rejection results in depression, anxiety, and a decrease in positive motivation to join groups (Leary, 1990). Thus, the outcome of extensive peer rejection and peer victimization is both negative and long term.

Most of this work, however, has been conducted from an individual social deficit model (Hymel, Wagner, & Butler, 1990). From that perspective, the focus of research is on the social deficits of the rejected child and/or the child who victimizes other children, as sometimes children who are rejected by others become victimizers (this relationship is complex and has been the focus of recent work in the area of peer harassment; see Graham & Juvonen, 2001). A range of risk factors that have been identified for children who victimize others includes aggressiveness (Hymel, Bowker, & Woody, 1993), the misreading of social cues (Crick & Dodge, 1994), and the inability to use prosocial strategies when responding to interpersonal conflicts (Crick & Dodge, 1989; Rubin & Krasnor, 1986). Factors that lead certain children to be rejected from groups include social withdrawal and shyness (Parkhurst & Asher, 1992), and social wariness (Newcombe & Bukowski, 1984). Researchers have recently pointed to the need to distinguish different subtypes of rejected children, those who are withdrawn and submissive from those who are aggressive (Rubin et al., 1998). More recently, researchers have pointed to the need to examine the relationship between children's social and moral judgments and victimization (see Arsenio & Lemerise, 2001). Generally, the individual social deficit model has led to interventions aimed at altering the behavior and thoughts of the rejected child (see Coie & Koeppl, 1990).

We propose that rejection from social groups requires an examination of the role that social groups play in addition (and sometimes in contrast) to the process of the individual social deficit model that currently predominates research in developmental psychology. From our perspective, there needs to be a close examination of decisions by social groups, and an analysis of the contexts in which individuals as members of groups reject others. There may be times when groups reject individuals for reasons that are wholly external to the social skills or social abilities of the individual being rejected. These reasons include group membership, such as gender, ethnicity, race, religion, and social class. Throughout history, in fact, social groups have excluded individuals who do not conform to the expectations of the group, and these expectations reflect criteria regarding group membership, such as gender, race, and ethnicity. This type of rejection is not a result of the individual child's lack of social skills but is an outcome of concerns about group functioning, which in many circumstances includes prejudice and stereotypic attitudes on the part of the members of the group. Although they are closely related, we distinguish this group functioning form of exclusion from relational aggression, which is defined as the *intent* to harm another by undermining inclusion in groups (see Crick & Grotpeter, 1995). Exclusion from groups is not necessarily a negative intent to harm others because there are situations in which exclusion from groups is designed to promote positive social group functioning without a negative intent toward others (e.g., exclusion of a slow runner from a sports team) as well

3

as to increase the comfort level of the group. Thus, without an examination of how children evaluate such acts, it is difficult to infer motives and intentions (see also Arsenio & Lemerise, 2001).

To formulate our theoretical model and to design our studies, we have drawn from an extensive body of literature on intergroup relationships in social psychology as well as on theory and research in developmental psychology. We have used a developmental social-cognitive model to formulate our hypotheses and expectations. We will now turn to our developmental model and then discuss theory and research on intergroup relationships, followed by a discussion of our prior studies on social reasoning about exclusion and inclusion, and conclude with a statement about our goals and expectations, which is expanded on in the next chapter.

SOCIAL-COGNITIVE DOMAIN MODEL

In the present project we analyze children's and adolescents' social reasoning about exclusion using a social-cognitive domain model (Turiel, 1983, 1998). The social-cognitive domain model guided this project in a number of ways. First, it provided a theoretical approach for analyzing social knowledge. Research generated from this model has provided a wealth of information on children's and adolescents' fairness reasoning (morality), social-conventional expectations (societal knowledge), and personal decision-making (psychological knowledge) (see Killen & Hart, 1995; Smetana, 1995; Turiel, 1983, 1998, 2002; Turiel, Killen, & Helwig, 1987). Three domains of knowledge have been identified: (a) the moral (justice, fairness, rights, and equality); (b) the societal (customs, conventions, norms, and etiquette); and (c) the psychological (individual jurisdiction, autonomy, self-esteem, and self-development). In general, the findings have revealed that individuals from early childhood to adulthood apply these forms of reasoning to their evaluations of social events, issues, and transgressions in social life. These categories were used to analyze how children and adolescents evaluated exclusion in multiple contexts in this study.

Second, our conceptualization of context stems from the social-cognitive domain model. A fundamental part of this project was to examine the ways in which children's and adolescents' reasoning about exclusion varies by the context—specifically, how exclusion is evaluated differently in situations that vary in terms of relationships and social expectations. The social-cognitive domain model proposes that individuals apply different forms of reasoning to a range of situations. This is in contrast to traditional stage models, which assume that individuals, at a particular point in their ontogenetic development, apply the same form of reason-

4

ing (referred to as a *structure*) across situations. From the social-cognitive domain perspective, it is proposed that individuals may apply reasons from one domain (e.g., moral or social-conventional) or more than one domain (both moral and personal) and that judgments include interpretations of specific features of the situation (see Helwig, 1995, 1997; Turiel et al., 1987, for analyses of context from this model). This approach is contextual in the sense that individuals' interpretations of context becomes part of their evaluation, and may be related to the type of reasoning that is applied to the situation. In this project, we predicted that evaluations of exclusion would vary depending on the context.

We chose to examine three contexts of exclusion judgments: friendship, peer group, and school; and two targets of exclusion: gender and race, resulting in six scenarios described to each participant. Our rationale for choosing these contexts and our expectations are described below. Because the social-cognitive domain model is context-oriented rather than stage-oriented, predictions are made about the multiple forms of reasoning that individuals use when assessing situations.

Third, researchers from the social-cognitive domain model have provided an established methodology for evaluating social reasoning about a wide range of issues and we applied this methodology in this project as well as extended it in several ways (to be discussed in more detail below). This includes using well-established coding systems for categorizing participants' reasons for their judgments and administering counterprobes for assessing the stability of children's and adolescents' judgments about exclusion.

Thus, the social-cognitive domain model guided this project by providing a conceptual basis for assessing social reasoning, a set of hypotheses about context, and a methodology for documenting children's and adolescents' social perspectives about exclusion. We now turn to a more in-depth description of the model.

In general, the strengths of the social-cognitive domain model, which have provided a striking contrast to the stage theories of moral development that were dominant until the early 1980s (Kohlberg, 1969, 1971, 1984; Piaget, 1932), are that (a) it analyzes the multiple forms of reasoning present in children's and adolescents' judgments rather than solely focusing on moral reasoning; (b) it moves the analysis away from how children and adolescents reason about unfamiliar hypothetical scenarios (sometimes once-in-a-lifetime events) to one that studies reasoning about everyday, familiar issues; (c) it examines how an individual's reasoning varies across a wide range of social contexts rather than reflecting general, global stages theorized to apply across diverse social contexts; (d) it shifts the focus of the study of morality away from the test of a hierarchical, primitive-to-advanced theory and toward an examination of how individuals coordinate different forms of reasoning, moral and nonmoral, at different points in development; (e) it allows for examination of contextual and cultural variation in moral and nonmoral social reasoning; and (f) it does not compare individuals from different cultures on one scale or "standard" (for reviews, see Helwig, 1995; Helwig & Turiel, 2002; Killen, 1991; Nucci, 2001; Smetana, 1995; Tisak, 1995; Turiel, 1983, 1998, 2002; Turiel et al., 1987).

Initially, researchers from the social-cognitive domain perspective examined how children reasoned about straightforward moral transgressions such as unprovoked hitting (Nucci & Turiel, 1978; Smetana, 1984) or refusing to share toys or take turns (Smetana, 1989b), and social-conventional transgressions such as refusing to line up for recess (Tisak, 1995) or violating mealtime etiquette (Davidson, Turiel, & Black, 1983). This was done to validate the proposition that individuals differentiate between rules that are morally based and those that pertain to social conventions. Researchers, beginning with Nucci (1981), then extended the model to examine how children evaluate issues that are not regulated by rules, such as choice of friends (Smetana & Bitz, 1996), choice of occupation (Bregman & Killen, 1999), and privacy (Nucci, 2001; Nucci & Herman, 1982)—issues that were categorized as part of the personal or psychological domain (Nucci, 1981, 1996). Most of these transgressions (moral or social-conventional) and issues are categorized as straightforward because individuals use predominantly one form of reasoning when evaluating the legitimacy and nature of the acts. For example, hitting is typically viewed as wrong because it hurts someone (e.g., the wrongfulness of inflicting harm on another), not sharing toys is conceptualized as wrong because someone is denied access to resources, and choosing a friend is perceived to be a personal choice decision.

Social-cognitive domain research in the past 10 years has moved from its initial focus on straightforward rule transgressions to investigating complex issues. In contrast to straightforward rule transgressions, complex issues typically involve the use of more than one form of reasoning to evaluate the nature of the act. The research has included investigating how individuals evaluate issues such as drug use (Nucci, Guerra, & Lee, 1991), religion (Nucci & Turiel, 1993), homosexuality (Turiel, Hildebrandt, & Wainryb, 1985), parent-adolescent conflict (Smetana, 1989a), mixed emotions (Arsenio & Fleiss, 1996; Arsenio & Lover, 1995), conflict resolution (Ardila-Rey & Killen, 2001; Killen & Sueyoshi, 1995), interpersonal responsibilities (Miller & Luthar, 1989), autonomy (Nucci, 2001), and cultural expectations of social norms (Killen & Wainryb, 2000; Nucci, Killen, & Smetana, 1996; Turiel & Wainryb, 1998; Wainryb & Turiel, 1994).

Findings resulting from this research have revealed that when individuals evaluate such acts and issues, they weigh different considerations and give priority to one perspective (or form of reasoning) over another. For example, in her research on adolescent-parent conflict, Smetana (1988) demonstrated that issues which generate conflict are ones in which adolescents and parents use different forms of reasoning to evaluate the same phenomenon. Adolescents judged cleaning one's room as a *personal* issue ("It's my room and I can live in it how I want to") and parents viewed it as a *social-conventional* issue ("If the neighbors see the way you keep this room I'll be embarrassed"). Nucci and Turiel (1993) examined how children and adolescents evaluate religious rules and prescriptions. They found that religious rules were evaluated with multiple forms of reasoning: moral (what one should do to be a good person), social-conventional (forms of dress and rituals that vary by religion), and personal (the decision to be a religious person). Thus, there are different ways in which issues can be complex. A complex issue may be one that some individuals view as a personal issue and others view as a social-conventional issue, such as certain examples of parent-adolescent conflicts. On the other hand, a complex issue may also be one in which most people use multiple forms of reasoning, such as moral, social-conventional, and personal ones, to evaluate it, as in the case of how people evaluate many religious prescriptions (Nucci & Turiel, 1993).

A small but burgeoning area of research from the social-cognitive domain perspective has focused on how individuals make judgments about democracy and rights (Helwig, 1997, 1998; Prencipe & Helwig, 2002; Ruck, Abramovitch, & Keating, 1998), tolerance (Crystal, Watanabe, & Chen, 2000; Wainryb, Shaw, & Maianu, 1998), personal freedoms (Nucci & Lee, 1993), acts of subversion and gender oppression (Turiel, 1998, 2002), and minority perspectives on autonomy and rights (Smetana & Gaines, 1999). These issues are complex because they involve the coordination of fairness and rights with judgments about social group, customs, norms, conventions, and personal choice. These foci are closely related to issues about exclusion based on group membership because exclusion potentially involves considerations of rights, tolerance, cultural expectations, social norms, and historical patterns of societal intergroup relationships. Only a few studies from the social-cognitive developmental model, however, have explicitly examined reasoning about intergroup relationships, such as reasoning about stereotypes, discrimination, and exclusion. We now discuss how the social-cognitive domain model has provided a way of examining context and a methodology for doing so.

The primary method used to investigate how individuals evaluate social issues from the social-cognitive domain model has been the interview method. Theoretical criteria have been used to examine whether individuals differentiate among social domains, and the types of justification responses given by individuals. For example, Turiel (1983) proposed that moral rules differ from social-conventional rules along a number of dimensions. These included (a) generalizability (Is the act wrong in another country or school?); (b) authority contingency (Is the wrongfulness of an act contingent on authority mandates?); (c) authority jurisdiction (Is it okay for parents/teachers/or the government to make rules about X?); (d) rule contingency (Is the act all right if there are no rules about it?); (e) rule alterability (Is it all right to change the rule?); and (f) punishment mandate (Is the act wrong if there is no punishment?). Turiel (1983, 1998) based these criteria on ones used by moral philosophers (see Gewirth, 1978; Nagel, 1979) and predicted that individuals would use these criteria to distinguish moral transgressions from social-conventional transgressions. Thus, one of the goals of the empirical project was to determine whether philosophical criteria reflect the ways in which individuals make distinctions between social and moral transgressions. Individuals were asked to give reasons for their classification and evaluation of acts. These reasons were coded into a wide range of categories, such as fairness, rights, equality, social conventions, authority, punishment avoidance, and personal choice.

Research conducted over the past two decades has supported the theoretical predictions about the use of criteria and justifications. In more than 90 empirical studies (see Tisak, 1995; Smetana, 1995; Turiel et al., 1987) it has been shown that children, adolescents, and adults identify moral rules as generalizable (not a matter of authority jurisdiction or contingency, not rule contingent, and not a matter of punishment). Conversely, social-conventional rules are viewed as context-specific (under authority jurisdiction, contingent on authority, rule contingent, and legitimate even if no punishment is involved). Studies on this difference have been conducted with children as young as $2\frac{1}{2}$ years of age (Smetana & Braeges, 1990) up through adulthood (Turiel et al., 1985). When asked about unprovoked hitting, for example, children say that it is wrong even when a teacher says it is all right, or when everyone in the class agrees it is all right, or when people in another country say it is all right. Yet, while children initially say that "wearing pajamas to school" is wrong, they judge the act as all right if the teacher says it's all right, and okay if everyone agrees to do it, and all right in another country (Tisak & Turiel, 1984). Thus, there has been empirical verification of the use of these theoretical criteria for determining the distinctions individuals make when evaluating moral and social-conventional transgressions.

Nucci formulated additional criteria to be used for determining when individuals believe that an issue is not a matter of regulations or rules but a matter of personal jurisdiction (Nucci, 1981, 2001). For example, children were asked to categorize acts as independent of authority (moral), contingent on authority (social-conventional), and not a matter of right or wrong but up to the individual to decide. Nucci found that children, adolescents, and parents identified a number of issues as personal, including choice of friends, hair length, clothes, and hobbies. This aspect of social reasoning has been documented in young children's judgments (Nucci, 2001) and in adolescent reasoning (Smetana & Bitz, 1996), as well as in parental judgments of children's role in the home (Nucci, 2001). Reasoning about the personal domain has also been shown to be important in judgments by individuals in non-Western cultures (Ardila-Rey & Killen, 2001; Nucci, Camino, Milintsky-Sapiro, 1996). Initially, these criteria were used to investigate how individuals evaluate straightforward issues, such as unprovoked hitting and conventional customs like etiquette; more recently they have been applied to complex issues involving a wide range of social contexts.

The social-cognitive domain model proposes that social reasoning varies by the context. In each situation, individuals have to assess the multiple dimensions often present in a context in order to make an evaluation, referred to as a *context analysis*. In most cases, individuals mentally pull apart the different dimensions of a situation and determine what predominates, what gets priority. Thus, it is essential for researchers to similarly analyze a situation being presented to participants for their evaluation. What are the components of the context and what are the predictions about how individuals will analyze it? The domain model provides some guidance. Are there moral components (e.g., issues of fairness, justice, or rights?), societal components (e.g., customs, cultural expectations?), and personal components (e.g., personal choice, privacy, intimate relationships?)? Additionally, Wainryb (1991) has indicated that many situations involve informational assumptions (judgments about reality, the nature of learning, etc.) that enter into evaluations of social contexts.

EVALUATING EXCLUSION

Studying Context

In this project, we identified three social contexts, friendship, peer group, and school, and made predictions about the forms of reasoning that individuals would use when evaluating exclusion in these contexts. The extensive literature on peer rejection and peer victimization has focused primarily on friendship relationships (Graham & Juvonen, 1998; Rubin et al., 1998). The friendship context is clearly one in which children experience exclusion and experience negative consequences as a result of these experiences. Research from the social-cognitive domain approach has shown that individuals use personal reasoning when discussing choice of friends and decisions about friendship relationships (Nucci,

1996). No research that we know of has examined how children evaluate exclusion of a friend based on arbitrary categories, such as race and gender. Do children view this as a personal decision because it is about friendship, or as a moral transgression because it is about treating someone in such a way as to hurt their feelings (psychological harm) or using unfair reasons for refusing to get to know them (prejudicial treatment)?

The second context we chose to examine was the peer group context. This context involves exclusion at the group level, which is distinct from the dyadic friendship context. Social groups emerge during childhood and peak during middle-school and high school (Brown, 1989). In middle school, students spontaneously organize themselves into cliques and groups with clearly defined members, rituals, and customs (Brown, 1989; Youniss & Smollar, 1985). Though structured group interactions are present in elementary school (e.g., sports, music clubs, chess clubs), adults organize most of these interactions, and parents and teachers govern membership. Exceptions occur during recess on the playground when exclusion from groups begins to occur. As has been documented by Putallaz and Wasserman (1990) entry into peer groups involves complex rituals that are slowly acquired by children through extensive group interaction. Research on entry rituals has shown that children who are excluded from groups are often those who have not yet figured out how to enter groups by using rituals that make it possible to join the group in a seamless fashion. This focus on the excluded child is important for understanding the consequences of peer rejection.

Children conceptualize social groups in social-conventional terms, such as focusing on what makes a group work well (group functioning; see Turiel, 1983). Children's behavior indicates that entry and exit rituals are created at a young age (by preschool) to give their social groups a sense of cohesiveness (Killen, 1991; Putallaz & Wasserman, 1990). What happens when a child uses entry rituals established by a peer group and continues to be rejected for reasons based on group membership, such as gender or race? The consequences of this type of rejection are not well understood, and one way to begin to understand this phenomenon is to study how children evaluate exclusion from groups based on gender and race. As Turiel (1983) articulated, social conventions are behavioral regularities designed to promote the smooth functioning of social groups. Most behavioral regularities are shared by members of groups (such as greetings, assigned roles, and shared group goals); yet, when conventions have to do with criteria for group membership itself, then the behavioral regularities designed to promote the group functioning may not be enough. For example, in the adult world, social conventions continue to exist that determine group membership, such as in golf clubs that are male-only. Interviews with male members of male-only golf clubs refer to social tradition and custom ("It's always been that way"; "It's what the members are comfortable with"). How early do these types of justifications emerge regarding group membership and exclusion? When do fairness and equality principles take priority over group tradition? This was the focus, in part, of the analyses, on the peer group context. When and how do children reason about exclusion from peer group contexts in social-conventional (in contrast to moral) terms? Thus, these two contexts, friendship and peer group, are quite different from our third context, the school setting, which is the predominant institutional context in the child's world.

Exclusion from a societally organized institution, such as school, has been studied extensively in adult populations (Minow, 1990; Opotow, 1990; Skrentny, 1996). Attitudes and conventions around race-segregated and gender-segregated schools have changed dramatically in the United States over the past century. The Brown v. Board of Education ruling in 1955 changed the legal basis for segregation, and with the Civil Rights Act of 1964, adult attitudes about exclusion based on race significantly changed by the end of the last century. Social psychologists have documented the ways in which explicit racism has significantly declined over the past 50 years in the United States (Dovidio & Gaertner, 2000), and this has been reflected in the condemnation of race-segregated institutions. Although it has not been the subject of extensive research, one would predict that most children also condemn such practices, viewing it as wrong from a strictly moral viewpoint.

Attitudes about gender-segregated institutions are more positive than are those about race-segregated institutions given that many institutions remain gender-specific (such as same-sex schools, Boy Scouts, Girl Scouts). At the same time, there is also a clear understanding in childhood that all children, boys and girls, should (and have the right to) attend school. Thus, we expected that the school context, one in which girls or African-American children were excluded from attending school, would be viewed very differently from the friendship and peer group contexts. Social institutions are subject to legal regulations and principles, which provide a more general level of accountability when it comes to the treatment of persons (Turiel, 1983). As a contrast to the friendship and peer group settings, we chose the school context as a setting in which exclusion was expected to be viewed in moral terms (as a moral transgression) and thus would be differentiated from dyadic and peer group forms of interaction, which would be viewed using multiple forms of reasoning.

Examining Gender and Race

In addition to context, we focused on two targets of exclusion: gender and race. We chose these two categories because individuals have

11

been excluded on the basis of gender and race more than any other group membership category (but not solely as a function of these categories; for example, other group membership categories such as religion, handicapped, body size, and nationality have also been the source of exclusion throughout the world; see Minow, 1990). For children living in the United States, gender and race are highly salient features of individuals that are the sources of stereotypic expectations as well as categorization, exclusion, bias, and discrimination (for research on gender see Ruble & Martin, 1998; for race, see Fisher, Jackson, & Villarruel, 1998).

Gender and racial categories of persons are similar because these categories are not chosen but given (see Fisher et al,. 1998). There are clearly significant differences in these two forms of exclusion, however, and this is a result, in part, of the different patterns of social behavior based on gender and race, and the different histories of oppression, discrimination, and stereotypes (Aboud & Amato, 2001). Whereas most U.S. citizens in most contexts explicitly condemn racial segregation, gender segregation is accepted in various contexts. Based on children's experiences and adult societal messages, we predicted that exclusion based on race would be viewed as more wrong than exclusion based on gender. Yet little is known regarding how children from different ethnic backgrounds evaluate racial exclusion in contrast to gender exclusion. This is due, in part, to the historical pattern of developmental research, which has only recently included children from different ethnic backgrounds in research studies.

Importance of Ethnicity

Over the past decade, developmental researchers have expanded their studies to include diverse ethnic minority populations. Initially, many of these research studies were conducted in such a way that minority groups, especially African-Americans in the United States, were compared to the "standard" or "control" represented by the majority group, European-Americans (Fisher et al., 1998; McLoyd & Randolph, 1986). McLoyd and Randolph (1986) referred to this approach as the "race comparative paradigm" and argued that the limitation of such an approach is that non-European-American populations have been understood only in reference to European-Americans, and not on their own terms. This has often been the case because much of the preliminary research on minority populations focused on the developmental deficits that exist for minority children living in North America. For example, developmental outcomes for minority children living in adverse conditions are compared to the developmental outcomes for majority children living in more advantaged circumstances. One of the reasons for this type of focus stems from the confound of socioeconomic status and race that exists in North America. In the United States, for example, African-Americans have disproportionately been in the lowest socioeconomic brackets (Fisher et al., 1998; Graves, 2001). As minority populations have moved out of poverty, however, and as North America has become more diverse with a wider range of ethnic minority communities, research has expanded beyond the race comparative paradigm. In addition, research has begun to examine the role of culture on development as well as on intergroup processes.

In this study, we interviewed children and adolescents from four ethnic backgrounds: African-American, European-American, Asian-American, and Latin-American. We refer to our participant groups by ethnicity because recent theorizing and research on culture and race have concluded that there is "no biological basis for separation of human beings into races . . . the idea of race is a relatively recent social and political construction" (Graves, 2001, p. 1). The conditions under which "racial groups" would be used would be when there is enough genetic differentiation among human beings to form a subspecies, and given that there is not enough genetic differentiation to form subspecies it is not wholly accurate to refer to people by their racial group even though this is common practice in many parts of the world and certainly in the United States. Generally, it is more consistent with biological research findings to refer to people along their ethnic origins rather than their racial makeup. However, racism along color lines exists in most of the world today, and it is color that is used to make decisions about exclusion as well as to pre-judge individuals in terms of their psychological character, motivation, morality, and intelligence (Banton, 1998; Fisher et al., 1998; Graves, 2001; Loury, 2002). Thus, we refer to our participants in terms of ethnicity, and we refer to our stimuli examples in terms of race (Black child; White child). Recent research with adolescents has also shown that adolescents, themselves, use the terms *race* and *ethnicity* interchangeably and do not differentiate between these labels in their discussions of identity and social groups (Ruck & Wortley, 2002).

Surprisingly, research on how children and adolescents from different ethnic backgrounds evaluate exclusion has been very minimal. Most of the research on prejudice has focused on the majority group's attitudes, and in the United States this refers primarily to European-American children's judgments (for a review, see Aboud & Amato, 2001). This is due in part to the concern that most forms of prejudice lie with the majority group's behavior toward minority groups. Research with minority children has typically focused on in-group bias and ethnic identity. Findings on in-group bias with minority children are mixed with some studies showing that young minority children display biases toward the out-group (e.g., African-American children display a "pro-White" bias) and

13

that this diminishes by 7 to 10 years of age (Katz & Kofkin, 1997). Ethnic identity has been positively related to successful intergroup relationships (Phinney, Cantu, & Kurtz, 1997), and studies have shown that minority children report more cross-race friendships than do European-American children (Aboud & Amato, 2001). Minority adolescents often experience discrimination in multiple settings as measured by self-report questionnaires (Fisher, Wallace, & Fenton, 2000). Together, these findings suggest that minority children would view exclusion of individuals based on group membership as wrong, particularly because they have experienced exclusion due to their ethnicity. Further, the experience of intergroup relationships has been one of the most significant predictors of a reduction in prejudice (Pettigrew & Tropp, 2000). Other studies with minority populations have typically focused on motivation and academic achievement, and how minority children's perceptions of victimization and harassment hinder their academic success and social adjustment (Graham & Juvonon, 1998). In general, we were interested in determining how children from different backgrounds evaluate exclusion based on group membership, and whether the experience of being a minority differentially influences how exclusion is evaluated.

CONCEPTUALIZATIONS OF EXCLUSION

In social psychology, exclusion has been conceptualized as a moral transgression (Opotow, 1990; Staub, 1987, 1990). Opotow defined *moral exclusion* as "when individuals or groups are perceived as outside the boundary in which moral values, rules, and considerations of fairness apply" (p. 1). Moral exclusion ranges from mild (passive unconcern) to severe (genocide) cases, but in all instances, it refers to instances in which one group perceives another group as "psychologically distant, expendable and undeserving" (p. 2). Opotow drew on Staub's (1990) theorizing in which he identified the psychological sources that contribute to acts of moral exclusion. Staub addressed the question of how it comes to be that one group so violently excludes another group. He examined the types of individual motivations and personal goals that can lead to acts of exclusion. Thus, that work focused on defining exclusion as solely moral, and investigating the psychological roots of such extreme behavior.

In addition to social psychology, legal theory also describes exclusion as a moral construct (see Minow, 1990). Minow, a legal theorist, stated that "the particular labels often chosen in American culture can carry social and moral consequences while burying the choices and the responsibility for those consequences" (p. 4). Traditional legal rules assume that there are boundaries between individuals and all others, and that these bound-

14

aries are distinct. Minow argued that there has been a price to pay for these legal distinctions, and that the most marginal and vulnerable members of society, such as women and children, pay the cost. In general, Minow's analysis focused on how the law treats differences and boundaries between people. She proposed a social-relational view in which individuals strive to take the viewpoint of others who are labeled "different." In her view, "a rights analysis may challenge the exclusion of 'different' people from schools and workplaces, but it fails to supply a basis for remaking those institutions to accommodate difference" (p. 377). Minow argued that reciprocal realities allow us to take the perspective of others and understand the need for inclusiveness. Though she did not reject an individual rights framework for solving problems of exclusion, she asserted that it is also necessary to invoke a social-relational perspective to correct social problems stemming from exclusion. Thus, research in social science and the law has typically assumed exclusion to be a moral transgression and has examined, in detail, the negative consequences for those excluded.

Our approach is different from the approaches of social psychology and legal theory because we are interested in the social cognition of exclusion—that is, how individuals conceptualize exclusion in a wide range of contexts. These other perspectives have been influential, however, in directing us to look for the types of justifications and reasons that individuals use to support or reject exclusion. We have found that there are contexts in which individuals view exclusion as a moral transgression in the way that Opotow or Minow framed it. Children and adolescents refer to the unfairness that occurs when someone excludes someone based on group membership, and the negative consequences such exclusion has for social interaction. We also found that there are situations in which individuals view exclusion as necessary for group functioning and for preserving cultural traditions and norms. These nonmoral social forms of reasoning need further inquiry. What does it mean to preserve group functioning or cultural traditions? Is it all right to preserve group functioning if the result is discrimination or if others think that it's wrong to exclude someone? When is preserving group functioning a guise for stereotypes or implicit biases about others who are different from the self? Developmental research has shown that an understanding of group functioning and social conventions increases with age (Turiel, 1983). Does this emerging knowledge bear on decisions about exclusion and inclusion? We designed the study in this *Monograph* to determine the extent to which individuals' use of criteria for evaluating social acts such as conventions and cultural norms applies to their judgments about exclusion from social groups. Thus, whereas Opotow's work concentrated on the psychological sources of moral inclusion, we focus on the multiple forms of social reasoning that are used to justify or reject exclusion.

Minow's work on exclusion argued for a social-relational perspective on rights. We have found that individuals also consider the *nature of the social relationship*, and the consequences to others in terms of interpersonal contact and treatment. Children often discuss their rejection of exclusion in terms of empathy and focus on the feeling states of individuals who are rejected. This supports Minow's argument that the social-relationship should (and has to be) considered when decisions about inclusion and exclusion are made. In contrast to Minow's model, however, we also find that many individuals discuss the issue of personal jurisdiction—they contend that a decision about friendship is a personal choice even if the reason that someone rejects someone as a friend is based on race or gender. Thus, social-relationships are brought into the process of decision-making about exclusion but not necessarily from the moral perspective. There are times when individuals view decisions concerning social relationships as a personal choice, not a matter of moral principles about how one should treat others. Because we are focused on the forms of reasoning that individuals use to evaluate exclusion, our research agenda is different from Minow's orientation, which is a legal interpretation of decisions about exclusion. Overall, our prior findings have revealed that children, adolescents, and adults reject exclusion based on gender and race in straightforward exclusion contexts and, at the same time, use social-conventional and personal reasoning to justify exclusion in complex or ambiguous situations. To formulate our hypotheses we drew on social psychological theory, which began investigating intergroup relations in the latter half of the 1900s.

Social Psychological Research on Stereotyping and Ingroup Bias

Following World War II, social psychologists conducted a close examination of the psychological basis for the emergence of stereotypes, prejudice, and in-group/out-group perceptions (Allport, 1954; Asch, 1952; Brewer & Brown, 1998; Dovidio, Kawakami, & Gaertner, 2000; Gaertner & Dovidio, 1986; Leyens, Yzerbyt, & Schadron, 1994; Mackie, Hamilton, Susskind, & Rosselli, 1996; Macrae, Stangor, & Hewstone, 1996; Oskamp, 2000; Tajfel & Turner, 1979). This work involved laboratory and simulated experiments using adult populations (college students and/or individuals in the workplace) and generated an expansive research program into many facets of attitudes, judgments, and beliefs about intergroup relationships. Most researchers defined *stereotypes* as overgeneralizations about social groups that take the form of attributions about individuals, and ignore intragroup variation (see Leyens et al., 1994; Mackie et al., 1996; Stangor & Schaller, 1996). These judgments reflected *cognitive structures*, which contain an individual's perception of knowledge, beliefs, and expectations about social groups (see Macrae et al., 1996). In general, the social psychology findings have shown that stereotypes are pervasive aspects of adult social attitudes, and that stereotypes are hard to change in adulthood (Stangor & Schaller, 1996).

Recently, social psychologists have also studied the mechanisms and strategies that contribute to the reduction of prejudice and discrimination (see Brown & Gaertner, 2001; Oskamp, 2000). *Prejudice* refers to negative biases toward others based on group membership. Studies on prejudice have revealed that although changing prejudiced attitudes is very difficult (Devine, Plant, & Buswell, 2000; Hamilton & Sherman, 1994), research on the conditions under which intergroup contact successfully reduces prejudice and discrimination has revealed positive findings (Allport, 1954; Pettigrew & Tropp, 2000). Allport's classic intergroup contact theory states that four optimal conditions must be met for intergroup contact to reduce prejudice: (a) equal status among the individuals; (b) common goals and opportunities for personal acquaintances; (c) intergroup cooperation; and (d) authority sanctioning of egalitarian intergroup interaction (social norms and expectations). Equal status refers to equal group status within the situation. The common goals condition refers to the notion that working toward achieving a common goal reduces prejudice, as with interracial sports teams in which the goal of winning overrides racial prejudice within the group. Intergroup cooperation means that the emphasis is on cooperation, not competition (see Sherif, 1966). Finally, positive intergroup attitudes are enhanced when those in authority sanction intergroup contact and relationships (see Pettigrew, 1998, for a review and discussion of these conditions). This authority includes teacher and school support for positive intergroup relationships as well as social norms, parental expectations, and societal approval of egalitarian principles.

Research within laboratory and field settings has generally found support for this set of conditions as instrumental in reducing prejudice and discrimination (see Gaertner, Rust, Dovidio, Bachman, & Anastasio, 1994). Further, social psychologists have formulated theoretical explanations for why these conditions work. Gaertner and colleagues (1994) proposed the Common Identity Ingroup Model to explain why intergroup contact, underspecific conditions, helps to reduce negative intergroup attitudes. The theory is that when individuals experience equal status, cooperative interactions, personalized contact, and supportive authority norms, their cognitive representation of *us versus them* changes to *we*. A common identity emerges that bridges in-group/out-group distinctions.

This work has relevance for our developmental research because it points to the sources of influence on intergroup attitudes, which include peer and authority expectations. Developmental research has pointed to the different roles that peers play on children's social development. What the social psychological findings and the intergroup contact theory research tell us is that peer and adult influences are also important sources that can potentially contribute to a reduction in biased intergroup attitudes. Thus, understanding how children view peer and adult influences (on judgments about exclusion) provides relevant information regarding the formation and the acquisition of intergroup biases. Further, the work on intergroup contact is relevant because it provides a set of variables that are important to examine when discerning the conditions that foster or reduce exclusion based on group membership.

Social psychological research has also shown that adults who make assumptions about others on the basis of race or gender also hold strong values about fairness and equality (Gaertner & Dovidio, 1986). Gaertner and Dovidio asserted that although most adults have strong beliefs about fairness, there are contexts in which exclusion based on race (or gender) is made implicitly, and individuals are often unaware that they hold these judgments. These contexts are ones in which there is some ambiguity about the features of the context. In straightforward situations involving decisions about others on the basis of race, for example, adults reject race as a reason to act or make a judgment. In ambiguous situations, however, in which the parameters of the situation are unclear, adults' stereotypes about others influence their decision-making. This has also been found to be the case with children and adolescents. When presented with ambiguous (McGlothlin, Killen, & Edmonds, 2002; Sagar & Schofield, 1980) or complex scenarios (Horn, Killen, & Stangor, 1999; Killen, Pisacane, Lee-Kim, & Ardila-Rey, 2001) children and adolescents sometimes resort to stereotypes when making social decisions. Gaertner and Dovidio (1986) believed that their findings point to the multiple perspectives held by adults regarding their evaluations of situations involving members of other groups. At times, equal treatment is granted, but, at times, differential treatment based on group membership is applied to the situation. Thus, these findings provide support for our expectation that children and adolescents use multiple forms of reasoning when evaluating exclusion based on gender and race.

Further, although explicit racism has decreased dramatically over the past several decades in the United States, implicit racism is still present (Dovidio & Gaertner, 2000; Gaertner & Dovidio, 1986). *Implicit racism* refers to unconscious biases that exist when individuals make decisions regarding members of stigmatized groups. We propose that implicit racism may be functioning, at times, when individuals evaluate exclusion. There are times when exclusion is justified by using nonmoral social reasons, such as group functioning and group identity. There are clearly times when these forms of reasoning are legitimate, but there may be other times when these orientations are a result of implicit biases. In order to test this theory, it is first necessary to analyze the extent to which individuals use nonmoral social reasons to justify exclusion in a range of contexts. This was one of the goals of the present study.

Developmental psychologists have turned their attention toward the topic of intergroup relationships, but only in the past decade or so, in contrast to a 50-year history of investigations by social psychologists using adult populations. We now turn to the developmental research on stereotypes and prejudice that provided guidance for our work.

Developmental Findings on Stereotyped Knowledge

Most of the prior work on children's intergroup attitudes has examined in-group biases (Bennett, Barratt, Lyons, & Sani, 1998; Bigler, Jones, & Lobliner, 1997), gender stereotypes (Katz & Ksansnak, 1994; Ruble & Martin, 1998), racial categories (Bigler & Liben, 1993; Hirschfeld, 1995) and prejudice (Aboud, 1988, 1992, in press; Aboud & Amato, 2001). These studies have been conducted using information processing models or cognitive-developmental models and have not approached the topic from a social-cognitive domain approach. Thus, these studies have not examined how children reason about the moral implications (fairness or unfairness) of making decisions that involve intergroup relationships and beliefs that reflect intergroup attitudes.

Research on children's stereotyped knowledge indicates that children begin recognizing and thinking about stereotypic expectations as early as the preschool years (Aboud, 1992; Bigler & Liben, 1993; Ruble & Martin, 1998). This includes children in North America (Ruble & Martin, 1998), Europe (see Bennett et al., 1998; Cairns, 1989), and the Mideast (see Bar-Tal, 1996; Cole et al., in press). Most of this evidence is based on either information processing models (Martin & Halverson, 1981; Stangor & Ruble, 1989), cognitive-developmental approaches (Aboud, 1988, 1992; Bigler & Liben, 1993), or social-cognitive models (Carter & Patterson, 1982; Killen & Stangor, 2001; Stoddart & Turiel, 1985). In this literature, stereotypes are defined as beliefs that children hold about others based solely on group membership. In the area of gender, stereotypes have been viewed as the shared beliefs about the typical characteristics of males and females (Martin, 1989; Ruble & Martin, 1998). From a social-cognitive domain model, however, stereotypes are one form of social-conventional reasoning (Stoddart & Turiel, 1985). This is because some stereotypes reflect expectations about what makes society function (social group functioning; see Stoddart & Turiel, 1985). This is particularly true of gender stereotypes (e.g., gender roles and activities) but it is also true of racial and ethnic stereotypes.

19

Gender stereotypes emerge early in development, prior to other forms of group stereotyping (such as race and ethnicity). For young children gender stereotypes include judgments about sex-appropriate activities (e.g., doll-playing for girls), sex-specific characteristics (e.g., boys are aggressive), and sex-related future roles (e.g., doctors are men; Ruble & Martin, 1998). Many studies have demonstrated that stereotypes influence children's memory and other social cognitive abilities (e.g., Carter & Patterson, 1982; Kuhn, Nash, & Brucken, 1978; Liben & Signorella, 1993; Martin & Halverson, 1981; Powlishta, 1995; Stangor & McMillan, 1992). For example, children have a better memory for information that is consistent with their gender stereotypes than for information that is inconsistent with gender stereotypes (Martin & Halverson, 1981), and the same is true for racial stereotypes (Bigler & Liben, 1993). Research has also shown that stereotypes affect the way in which children tell stories and acquire new information (Hirschfeld, 1995; Koblinsky, Cruse, & Sagawara, 1978; Martin & Halverson, 1981; Martin, Wood, & Little, 1990; Welch-Ross & Schmidt, 1996). These findings demonstrate that stereotypes reflect implicit as well as explicit forms of knowledge, and are difficult to change.

Stereotyping, like categorization, is one way to process information and to make sense of social phenomena. In the area of gender stereotypes, labels attached to males and females often stem from social-role expectations. Because of these role-related expectations, some forms of gender stereotyping are condoned more readily than are expectations about racial and ethnic stereotyping due to the complex sociopolitical histories and multifarious societal forces (Minow, 1990; Okin, 1989, 1999). Of relevance to our work is that stereotypes are a persistent form of knowledge that children use when making everyday social decisions.

Social-cognitive domain research on children's gender stereotypes has shown that gender-specific expectations reflect social-conventional rather than moral knowledge (Carter & Patterson, 1982; Stoddart & Turiel, 1985). For example, in the study by Stoddart and Turiel, children who stated that a boy wearing a hair barrette was wrong did so for social-conventional, not moral, reasons (e.g., "Boys who wear skirts look silly but it's okay if everyone does it"). Such gender stereotypes may reflect social-conventional reasoning, but no research that we know of has examined what forms of reasoning are applied to racial stereotyping. We predict that reasoning about actions that reflect racial exclusion may be social-conventional in that the exclusion is justified in terms of traditions and customs ("It's always been that way"); however, no research has specifically examined this issue. Although stereotypes may not reflect morally negative behavior toward others, the use of stereotypes in situations that involve treatment of others, such as denial of resources, is morally relevant. Social psychologists have demonstrated that adults' use of stereotyping often leads to prejudice (Mackie et al., 1996).

In a recent review of the research, Aboud and colleagues (Aboud, 1988; Aboud & Amato, 2001; Aboud & Levy, 2000) concluded that racial and ethnic attitudes are evident in early childhood. Young children's cognitive limitations make them more likely than older children to apply biases to the categorization of individuals on the basis of race. Research on racial stereotypes has found that, with age, children associate different characteristics and judgment with certain groups, and that racial attitudes affect children's behavior and choice of friends (Aboud, 1992). Typically, children's prejudice has been measured by the extent to which children assign negative and positive traits to individuals solely on the basis of their membership in a gender group or racial group (Aboud, 1992; Bigler & Liben, 1993). Older children become capable of assigning positive as well as negative traits to individuals of the out-group in contrast to younger children who can only assign one trait to a member of the out-group (Aboud, 1992). The result is that preschool children display an in-group bias because they assign positive traits to the in-group, and negative traits to the out-group (Aboud, in press).

Assigning multiple traits to individuals has been related to changes in cognitive development, such as the acquisition of classification and conservation skills (in which children become capable of simultaneously weighing multiple variables, such as length and width). These findings have led researchers to conclude that children's prejudice, or assigning of negative traits, declines with age, as they become capable of simultaneously weighing multiple variables (Aboud, 1992; Aboud, in press; Aboud & Levy, 2000; Doyle, & Aboud, 1995). Recent studies also have shown in-group and out-group attitudes to be reciprocally correlated in a sample of children from a homogeneous school but not in a sample from a heterogeneous school (Aboud, in press). This finding suggests that social experience with others who are different from the self enables children to differentiate between in-group favoritism and negative attitudes about the out-group. This is supported by intergroup contact findings in which experience with the out-group reduces prejudice (Pettigrew & Tropp, 2000).

Researchers have also examined other indices of prejudice, such as perceptions of within-group variability and between-group variability (Bigler et al., 1997), and evaluations of within-group similarity and dissimilarity (McGlothlin et al., 2002). This is necessary because, although the assignment of multiple traits increases with age indicating a reduction in prejudice (according to this measure), prejudicial judgments and behavior are nonetheless evident in adolescence and adulthood.

Social psychologists, who have extensively studied in-group/out-group perceptions, attitudes, and behavior in adults, have demonstrated

21

the out-group homogeneity effect (Park, Ryan, & Judd, 1992), whereby individuals recognize variability in their own group (the in-group) to a much greater extent than in other groups (the out-group). The out-group homogeneity effect potentially leads to stereotyping because the individual assumes that all members of the out-group share the same characteristics; thus labels are attributed to individuals in out-groups without a recognition of the heterogeneity within the out-group. There is a vast literature on judgments about in-group/out-group relationships in the adult social psychology literature (Brewer, 1979; Mackie et al., 1996; Tajfel, Billig, Bundy, & Flament, 1971), and less treatment of the issue by developmental psychologists (for exceptions, see Aboud, Mendolsohn, & Purdy, in press; Bennett et al., 1998; Bigler et al., 1997; Yee & Brown, 1992). When children ignore variations within groups and attribute labels based solely on group membership this may be the result of a lack of familiarity with the group (see McGlothlin, et al., 2002).

Depending on the context, decisions about inclusion and exclusion involve judgments that potentially reflect knowledge and biases about in-group/out-group relationships. Children may exclude others in the out-group because their assumption is that these individuals have characteristics that are undesirable or unfamiliar. As children have more contact with individuals from different social groups, however, they recognize the heterogeneity that exists within groups as evidenced by Aboud's (in press) recent findings on in-group/out-group judgments from children in heterogeneous and homogeneous school environments. This increased recognition of heterogeneity occurs at the same time that there is a decrease in rigidity in stereotypes about gender, suggesting that these two processes are related. However, very little research has been conducted with the goal of understanding the connection between the judgments of heterogeneity and moral reasoning. Given the extensive empirical documentation of the emergence of stereotyping in childhood, it is essential to examine how stereotypic knowledge is manifested when individuals make social and moral decisions that involve intergroup relationships.

PRIOR RESEARCH ON EXCLUSION

In our earlier research on social reasoning about exclusion, we proposed that exclusion is a complex issue that involves multiple forms of reasoning. We conducted a number of studies to examine the forms of reasoning brought to bear on decisions about inclusion and exclusion from groups. These studies were designed to integrate social psychological theory on stereotypes and prejudice with developmental psychology work on moral, social-conventional, and psychological reasoning, in order to examine how children and adolescents evaluate exclusion in multiple contexts (Horn et al., 1999; Killen, Crystal, & Watanabe, 2002; Killen, McGlothlin, & Lee-Kim, 2002; Killen et al., 2001; Killen & Stangor, 2001; Killen, Stangor, Price, Horn, & Sechrist, 2002; Lee-Kim, 2002; Theimer, Killen, & Stangor, 2001).

In these studies, we interviewed children about their evaluation of a group's decisions to exclude someone because of gender or race. For example, in one study we interviewed preschool-aged children (from three different ethnic groups, $N = 72$) about whether it was all right for (a) a group of girls playing with dolls to exclude a boy and (b) a group of boys playing with trucks to exclude a girl (Killen et al., 2001). This type of decision involves issues of fairness (Is gender a legitimate reason to exclude someone?) and psychological harm (Will someone feel bad for being excluded?) as well as stereotypic knowledge (Girls play with dolls and boys play with trucks). We interviewed children about their evaluation of exclusion ("Is it all right or not all right for the group to exclude the child who wants to join?"), as well as their evaluation of a more complicated decision ("Now there is only room for one child to join the group and both a boy and a girl want to join. Who should the group pick?"), for four types of activities: doll-playing, truck-playing, teacher role-playing, and firefighter role-playing.

Contrary to what might be predicted, given the strength of stereotypic associations of play activities and gender roles, the majority of children stated that it would be wrong to exclude someone in the straightforward condition (there were no differences for the gender or ethnicity of the participants). Children gave clear priority to fairness over stereotypes for all four contexts. Asking children about more complicated decisions, however, generated different judgments. In an inclusion decision condition ("Who should the group pick when there is only room for one to play?"), about half of the children picked someone who fit the stereotype (a girl to play with dolls or a boy to play with trucks) and used stereotypes to support their decision. The other half picked someone who did not fit the stereotype (a boy to play with dolls and a girl to play with trucks) and gave reasons based on equal opportunity and equal treatment. Thus, we concluded that children bring at least two forms of reasoning to bear on decisions about group inclusion and exclusion: fairness knowledge and stereotypic knowledge about gender activities.

Moreover, using a counterprobe technique we found that those children who chose a child to join the group based on a stereotype for the gender-related activities (dolls, trucks) were more likely to change their judgment after hearing a moral probe than were children who initially picked a child that did not fit the stereotype. This indicated that fairness ("What about picking Tom because boys don't usually get a chance to play with dolls?") was a more powerful probe than was a stereotype (What about picking Sally because girls usually play with dolls, not boys?"). This was true for boys and girls as young as $4\frac{1}{2}$ years of age. This study showed that young children bring different forms of reasoning to bear on inclusion and exclusion decisions; moreover, they are actively weighing and coordinating these forms of knowledge when making these types of decisions. Further, children as young as the preschool period are capable of rejecting gender-related stereotypes when making morally relevant decisions involving exclusion.

In a subsequent study with elementary and high school students, we examined judgments about exclusion based on gender and race (Killen & Stangor, 2001). We interviewed European-American children at 4th, 7th, and 10th grade levels ($N = 131$) about four types of inclusion and exclusion decisions for after-school peer group clubs: ballet (boy is excluded), baseball (girl is excluded), basketball (White child is excluded), and math club (Black child is excluded). Again, the vast majority of all children judged it wrong to exclude someone in the straightforward condition, and viewed exclusion based on race as more wrong than exclusion based on gender. In more complex situations, stereotypes emerged. When asked whom the group should pick when there was room for only one more child to join the group, stereotypic preferences took priority in the gender-related contexts. This was also true for the race-related contexts, but only with age (younger children did not use stereotypes about race to make these types of decisions). With age, we found that adolescents increasingly relied on group functioning reasons for choosing someone who fit the stereotype ("The group will work better with someone who is like the other members of the club"). Further, across all contexts, girls gave priority to fairness over stereotypes more so than did boys.

The findings from this study provide a picture of what is happening developmentally regarding decisions about inclusion and exclusion. Social knowledge about customs, conventions, and even stereotypes enters into adolescents' decision-making about inclusion. On the positive side, this shows their increasing knowledge about social group dynamics and group goals. On the negative side, this reveals ways in which stereotypes about others become incorporated into morally relevant decision-making. We have also found that females are much less likely to rely on stereotypes about others, and are much more likely to use fairness as a reason for including someone who does not fit a stereotype than are boys.

The gender finding, that girls view exclusion as more wrong than do boys, has been replicated in every study that we have conducted on social reasoning about exclusion, and deserves some comment. It could be argued that girls are more interpersonally oriented than are boys and this accounts for the gender finding. Yet girls' reasons for the wrongfulness of exclusion were based on fairness reasons, not empathy or kindness. In some gender work, interpersonal orientations have been contrasted to justice orientations (Gilligan, 1977). However, in our studies females use justice (as well as fairness, equality, and rights) as why someone should not exclude someone else solely as a function of group membership. This supports previous findings that have shown that both boys and girls use justice and care reasoning (Smetana, Killen, & Turiel, 1991). Surprisingly, we did not find any in-group biases. That is, girls rated exclusion of boys as equally wrong as exclusion of girls, and did so more than did boys (e.g., girls judged it more wrong for a girl to exclude a boy than did boys). This finding discounts a gender identity or in-group bias explanation.

We propose that the gender differences we have found in prior studies are a function, in part, of individuals' past experience with exclusion. Girls have experienced exclusion in the area of sports (traditionally) as well as other gender-related academic activities (math and science) and this may account for their sensitivity toward the wrongfulness of exclusion, rather than it having to do with being female per se. Another possibility is that girls' experience with relational aggression (Crick, 1997) makes them highly sensitive to the wrongfulness of exclusion, which is frequently a core part of what occurs when individuals relate to one another in nonphysical aggressive ways. In our studies, however, we do not equate exclusion based on group membership with relational aggression because we do not define exclusion as an intention to harm someone (see Crick & Grotpeter, 1995), as there are times when exclusion does not derive from an intent to harm someone but from an intent to make social groups work well.

One way to test our hypotheses about gender is to study how children, particularly boys, from other traditionally excluded groups evaluate acts of exclusion. We had expected to test this hypothesis in the Killen and Stangor (2001) study, but our number of African-American participants was too low to conduct statistical analyses for age and gender (N = 31 for males and females at 4th, 7th, and 10th grades). Based on overall comparisons, however, we found that African-Americans were less willing than were European-Americans to exclude a child from a group, and they were more likely to pick the child who did not conform to the stereotype than were European-Americans. Yet, due to the low frequencies we could not make generalizations about the role of the ethnicity of the participant on judgments about inclusion and exclusion. This issue, among many others, led us to formulate the present study by including systematic data on children from different ethnic backgrounds, evenly represented by age and gender of the participant for children from each background.

25

In our prior research we had not examined the role of external social influences on how children and adolescents evaluate exclusion. Do children view exclusion as wrong even when told that their peers think it is all right (social consensus)? Do children view exclusion as wrong even when parents say that it is all right (e.g., that it is not a matter of authority jurisdiction)? Do children view exclusion as wrong in diverse cultures (e.g., generalizable)? These factors—the roles of social consensus, authority influence, and cultural expectations—are investigated in the present project. Investigating how external influences affect children's social reasoning about exclusion provides essential information about the extent to which exclusion is viewed solely as a moral transgression or whether it is viewed as a matter of social consensus and authority mandates, and varies by cultural context (see Smetana, 1995; Tisak, 1995; Turiel, 1983). These sources of influence (referred to as criteria) have been used in social-cognitive domain research to demonstrate how children differentiate moral transgressions (e.g., hitting) from social-conventional transgressions (e.g., not standing in line for recess) and decisions involving personal choice (e.g., what to wear). In the present study, we examine how children reason about these sources of influence and we determine the extent to which children change their judgments as a function of external influence probes. These analyses provide information regarding the criteria children and adolescents use to evaluate exclusion decisions in multiple contexts as well as whether their judgments about exclusion are stable or subject to change as a function of external influences.

II: GOALS AND AIMS OF THE PRESENT PROJECT

In the study described in this *Monograph*, we have five goals: (a) to demonstrate that children and adolescents reason about exclusion differently in multiple contexts, specifically, friendship, peer group, and school (*the role of context*); (b) to examine differences that emerge in the way children evaluate gender and racial exclusion (*targets of exclusion*); (c) to reveal the roles played by social consensus, authority influence, and cultural expectations in how children make exclusion decisions (*sources of external influences*); (d) to assess whether children change their judgments as a function of external influences (*stability of judgments*); and (e) to determine the ways age, gender, and ethnicity of the participants are related to how exclusion is evaluated (*person and group membership variables*). We will discuss each of these goals in detail.

GOAL ONE: THE ROLE OF CONTEXT

Our past studies focused, for the most part, on evaluations of exclusion from peer group contexts (for either gender or race). Based on developmental findings that have demonstrated significant context effects for social judgments (Helwig, 1995), in the present study we included decisions about friendship relationships, peer groups, and societally based decisions to exclude others (specifically, from attending school). Context influences whether children view exclusion as a moral transgression or as a personal decision (see also Helwig, 1995; Killen et al., 2002) and also includes a number of factors that give an event social meaning. On the basis of prior findings by Helwig (1995, 1998) and our own studies we hypothesized that context would be a significant predictor of how children reason about exclusion. Little is known about how context is related to children's social reasoning about exclusion, and therefore three different contexts of exclusion were investigated in this study: friendship, peer group, and school.

In the present study, unlike in our past studies on exclusion, we did not use contexts that reflected stereotypic activities for children (e.g., girls excluded from baseball or White children from a Black basketball team; see Killen & Stangor, 2001). This was done for several reasons. First, our prior studies focused on peers, and the present study was designed to extend exclusion scenarios beyond the peer group, to friendship and institutional contexts. Peer groups are often gender-specific (ballet), and in a very few cases, are race-specific (basketball team), but this is not the case for friendship relationships. Further, institutions are often gender-specific (same-sex schools, Girl Scouts, Boy Scouts, fraternities, sororities) but are no longer race-specific. Interviewing children about exclusion from gender-specific institutions would constitute a very different project, and it would not be feasible to match up similar race-specific scenarios. Thus, we decided that for this study we would create a protocol in which we interviewed children about exclusion based on gender and race in nonstereotypic contexts: friendship, peer group, and school.

We formulated a set of predictions about the types of social reasoning children would use to evaluate exclusion in these three contexts. We predicted that evaluations of exclusion would involve multiple forms of reasoning for the peer group and the friendship contexts (moral and social-conventional for the peer group; moral and personal reasoning for the friendship context). We expected that, in contrast, for the school context students would use predominantly moral reasons (fairness, wrongfulness of discrimination, equal access). In this project, we differentiated among the types of reasons within each domain to determine whether these forms of reasoning vary for a complex issue like exclusion. For example, as shown in Table 1 (and defined below), the moral domain included reasons such as fairness, equality, rights, prosocial, and integration. The social-conventional domain included group functioning and group identity, social traditions and stereotypic expectations, authority, and peer pressure. The psychological domain included personal choice. These categories were derived from philosophical criteria (for morality, see Gewirth, 1978; Nagel, 1979; Roemer, 1998), from our prior research studies on exclusion (see Killen & Stangor, 2001), and from extensive pilot data.

In our prior studies we found that children and adolescents typically used moral (fairness) and social-conventional (group functioning) reasons (Killen & Stangor, 2001) to evaluate exclusion from peer groups. Because we expanded the contexts in the present study, we predicted that the range of reasons to justify or condemn acts of exclusion would widen as well. Thus, we predicted that children and adolescents would use a range of reasons, from personal (friendship) to group functioning (peer

TABLE 1

JUSTIFICATION CODING CATEGORIES

Category	Description
Moral	
Fairness	Appeals to the maintenance of fairness in the treatment of persons (e.g., "I think Jessica should be allowed in the music club because it's only fair that everybody should be able to be in the club"), the equal treatment of persons (e.g., "Everyone should be treated the same"), or the rights of the individual (e.g., "Let Amy go to school because everybody has a right to an education").
Empathy	Appeals to the feelings of the individual being excluded (e.g., "It is not nice to exclude someone"), and to the helping and caring about others by including them (e.g., "Jerry should be friends with Damon because Damon doesn't have any friends").
Integration	Appeals to wrongfulness of discrimination and the consequences of prejudice for the larger society or for humanity (e.g., "When people are prejudiced then no one can get along and it hurts everyone all over the world")
Social conventional	
Group functioning	Appeals to the need to make the group function well (e.g., "The club will be better"), to the identity of the group (e.g., "The white kids need their own club"), and the decision-making jurisdiction of the group to decide its members (e.g., "The group can decide whatever they want").
Social tradition	Appeals to traditions as well as labels attributed to an individual based on group membership and stereotypes (e.g., "Black kids like different music than white kids").
Authority	Appeals to parental jurisdiction, parental authority (e.g., "You have to obey your parents"), and governmental rules and laws (e.g., "If the government says it's okay, then it's okay, because you can't go against the government"). Includes negative consequences, such as punishment (e.g., "He might get in trouble if he hangs out with Damon").
Social influence	Appeals to the influence of others on whether or not to exclude the individual (e.g., "He should do what his friends say or he could lose their friendship").
Psychological	
Personal choice	Appeals to individual preferences or prerogatives (e.g., "Jerry can choose who his friends are").

group) and morality (school). On the basis of our prior studies we had expectations about the reasons children would give for making a judgment about exclusion that were related to the children's age and gender (this is discussed in more detail later).

GOAL TWO: GENDER AND RACIAL TARGETS OF EXCLUSION

In this *Monograph* study, we compared children's evaluations of exclusion based on race with their evaluations of exclusion based on gender. In past studies we used two-way exclusion protocols (boys exclude girls; girls exclude boys; black children exclude a white child; white children exclude a black child), but in the present study we used one-way exclusion scenarios and we described the same scenarios to all participants. In all of the scenarios, a member of the majority culture or dominant gender group (e.g., a White boy) excluded a member of a minority culture (Black boy) or the subordinate gender group (girl). We did not reverse the roles in the story to include a member of a minority group excluding a majority member or a girl excluding a boy. There were several reasons why we used a one-way exclusion design. First, in three prior studies in which we used two-way exclusion designs (for race: White group excludes a Black child, and Black group excludes a White child; for gender: girl group excludes a boy, and boy group excludes a girl) we did not find an in-group bias or differences between the types of exclusion within the same target (Killen & Stangor, 2001; Killen et al., 2001; Theimer et al., 2001). We did, however, find a target effect (exclusion based on race was viewed as more wrong than exclusion based on gender) and a gender-of-the-participant effect (girls viewed all forms of exclusion as more wrong than did boys). Certainly one study is not enough to thoroughly examine differences for the direction of exclusion within targets, but we did not find differences between the different types of exclusion when we pilot-tested our protocol for this study. Moreover, we had some decisions to make. Given that we wanted to focus on the context of exclusion (friendship, peer group, and school) and the target of exclusion (gender, race), and that we wanted to administer a number of dependent measures (evaluations of social consensus, authority, and generalizability) for participants at three grade levels, both male and female, and of different ethnicities, we would not have been able to administer two-way forms of exclusion to all participants for all combinations. Adding four ethnic groups made the project particularly complicated. We would have to generate 12 possible exclusion pairs and decide which version to administer to which group. As it was, we administered six scenarios to each child with 8 dependent measures per scenario. Given the lack of two-way findings in the previous study, and the lack of much information about context (all previous studies were done on the peer context) we decided to forgo the two-way form of exclusion in this project.

We believe that another methodology needs to be created to better understand two-way forms of exclusion. Clearly there are different implications if a White child excludes a Black child or a Black child excludes a

White child (the same for a boy excluding a girl and a girl excluding a boy). These are not purely reciprocal forms of exclusion. One type of exclusion repeats a history of discrimination and oppression in the United States and much of the world and the other type reflects either a form of reverse discrimination (according to some) or a statement about group identity (according to others). Sociologically, politically, and historically, these two forms of exclusion are quite different (Graves, 2001; Loury, 2002). For this project, however, we chose to standardize our interview by administering the same type of exclusion to all participants, and by using the form of exclusion that most readily typifies the experience of individuals in the areas of racial and gender exclusion. Keeping the form of exclusion constant allowed for generalizations about reasoning about discrimination against one ethnic group or gender group across all of our participants.

Our hypothesis about the target of exclusion was that gender exclusion would be more readily condoned than racial exclusion. Gender segregation is more explicitly accepted than racial segregation in most areas of current U.S. culture; furthermore, social messages geared to children about gender and race reveal that although gender segregation is purposefully encouraged (Bigler, 1995), racial segregation is directly discouraged (Nucci, 2001). Due to the explicit nature of our interview protocols, in which children were directly asked about exclusion based on gender and race, we expected that children's and adolescents' negative judgments about racial exclusion would be stronger than for gender exclusion given that gender-segregated interactions are often justified in social-conventional terms (Carter & Patterson, 1982) and racially segregated interactions are overtly condemned (particularly in the school environments experienced by children in this study).

GOAL THREE: EXTERNAL SOURCES OF INFLUENCE

We examined how children evaluated three sources of external influence on exclusion: social consensus, authority influence, and generalizability. These sources of influence were chosen because they have been used extensively in prior social-cognitive domain research to determine how children classify social acts and events (Tisak, 1995) and have been shown to be important aspects of children's social reasoning. First, we examined social consensus, defined as peer and cohort influence, because we theorized that peer influence was an important aspect of peer exclusion, and we predicted that this form of influence would be particularly salient in exclusion contexts. Stemming from Solomon Asch's (1952) classic work on group behavior and conformity, social psychological research

31

has examined the ways in which social consensus changes individuals' evaluations of social acts. Developmental psychologists have studied social consensus as a function of peer group pressure, particularly in adolescence (Brown, 1989). In this project, we distinguish social consensus from authority pressure and define social consensus as peer pressure or common status influence. Our social consensus assessment refers to whether the evaluation of the act of exclusion was influenced by another peer's recommendation. In this way, social consensus refers to an opposing decision from a group of other friends in the friendship context, other children who wanted to join the club in the peer group context, and other citizens in the school context.

We had several expectations about the conditions under which children would evaluate the legitimacy of exclusion as a function of social consensus or influence. We expected that social consensus would be salient to children as a function of the context, the age of the participant, and the target of exclusion. We varied the salience in each context such that in the friendship context, we asked children whether their exclusion decision would change if a friend recommended something different. For the peer group and school contexts, we asked children whether their evaluation of exclusion would change with a different decision from members of another music club (peer group) or from citizens in the town (school). From a social-cognitive domain perspective, it would be expected that social consensus would be relevant only for social-conventional, not moral events and transgressions. This is because social-conventional expectations stem from the group and are determined by group consensus in contrast to moral principles, which are independent from group expectations. Thus, the extent to which individuals would change their evaluation of exclusion as a function of social consensus would indicate one way in which the issue has nonmoral dimensions to it for the individual making the judgment.

Studies have shown that children's moral evaluations are not contingent on authority influence; that is, moral transgressions are viewed as wrong even when individuals in positions of authority (parents, teachers) view the act as all right (see Laupa, 1986; Smetana, 1995; Tisak, 1995). We expected that children's evaluations of exclusion would be influenced by authority figures in some contexts and not in other contexts. More specifically, we predicted that authority influence would bear on how children evaluated exclusion in the friendship and peer group context but not in the school context.

Prior studies have shown that children view moral transgressions as wrong in another culture (e.g., "hitting" is wrong anywhere) and that social-conventional transgressions are culturally specific (e.g., boys wear skirts in Scotland). We investigated how children evaluated the generalizability of excluding someone based on gender or race. Would it be all right in another culture? Children's evaluations of the generalizability of exclusion would provide information regarding their conceptualization of exclusion, as moral or social-conventional, and how this related to the context of exclusion. We predicted that children would judge exclusion in the friendship and peer group contexts as all right in other cultures but that disallowing girls or Black children to attend school would be wrong. Again, we predicted the generalizability of racial exclusion would be more pervasive in children's responses than the generalizability of gender exclusion.

GOAL FOUR: STABILITY OF EXCLUSION JUDGMENTS

In this study, we tested the extent to which children and adolescents changed their judgments when considering social pressure from peers, authority, and cultural norms (referred to as *external influence*). We designed this aspect of the study to determine the extent to which students would stick with their view that exclusion was wrong (or legitimate). We chose these three sources of external influence because they have been shown to be actual sources of influence on children's acquisition of prejudice (Aboud, 1992) and in-group biases (Aboud & Amato, 2001). Though peer influence has often been viewed in negative terms regarding children's social development (for a review, see Rubin et al., 1998), researchers have pointed to the positive sources of influences. For example, cross-race friendships are one of the most significant predictors of prejudice reduction (Pettigrew, 1998). Authority influence has also been shown to serve both positive and negative forms of influence on children's development. Socialization approaches often emphasize the importance of adult modeling on children's behavior (for a review, see Grusec & Goodnow, 1994); cognitive-developmental models often point to the limitations of adult forms of influence due to the unilateral nature of the adult-child relationships (for a review see Smetana, 1997). Finally, cultural norms have often been a source of influence as well in that cultural expectations are theorized as guiding social behavior (Greenfield & Cocking, 1994).

In one of our prior studies (Killen et al., 2001) we found that preschool-aged children changed their judgments when hearing fairness probes more often than when hearing stereotype probes. This was significant because it indicated that children did not change their judgment solely as a function of hearing any probe from an adult interviewer. If this were the case, then children would be as equally likely to change their judgment in the positive direction, from *all right* to *not all right* as

33

they would in the negative direction, from *not all right* to *all right*. How-ever, most preschool-aged children changed their judgment in only one direction, from *all right to exclude* (using stereotypes as a reason) to *not all right* (using fairness reasons) than the other way around. We interpreted this finding as evidence that children give a greater priority to fairness than to stereotypic knowledge when given the opportunity to weigh both types of considerations.

Thus, there were several expectations regarding children's responses to the three external probes. The first was that when children changed their judgments, they would change in only one direction, from condon-ing exclusion to rejecting it, and not the reverse, from viewing exclusion as wrong to viewing it as legitimate. Second, we predicted that exclusion based on the school context would be viewed predominantly in moral terms, leading children to reject all forms of external influence in con-trast to the friendship and peer group contexts in which responses would be mixed. Some children would change their judgments as a result of the external influence for friendship and the peer group and others would not. This would be based, in part, on the type of probe, with social con-sensus being more salient than authority, given the importance of peer relationships on intergroup relationships (see Aboud & Amato, 2001). We did not have specific expectations about the proportion of children who would change overall given the lack of prior evidence on this aspect of children's judgments.

GOAL FIVE: AGE, GENDER, AND ETHNICITY OF PARTICIPANTS

We chose our three age groups, 4th, 7th, and 10th graders, for several reasons. First, we did not want to interview children younger than 4th grade about exclusion based on race. There are mixed findings on the extent to which young children (kindergarten to 2nd grade) explicitly think about race when making social decisions (Aboud & Amato, 2001; Hirschfeld, 1995). We did not want to introduce this category to children if they did not already think about it when making morally relevant decisions, such as exclusion. Most of the findings indicate that children are aware of eth-nicity and race by 3rd grade. To be cautious we included 4th graders as our youngest age group. In addition, research has shown that young chil-dren have difficulty coordinating two variables simultaneously and this cognitive-developmental limitation is revealed in their inability to think about individuals in racial categories as having both positive and negative traits (Bigler & Liben, 1993). Because we did not directly assess cognitive ability, and it was not a focus of our study, we interviewed children who were clearly past the early stages of cognitive-development reasoning.

Social group functioning and knowledge about social norms increases during the early adolescent years (Brown, 1989; Horn, in press; Turiel, 1983; Youniss & Smollar, 1985) and social cliques and social reference groups peak at 9th grade (Youniss, McLellan, & Strouse, 1994). To cover this developmental phase of social cognitive perspective on groups, we interviewed children prior to, and after, the peak period in which social groups and cliques predominate social perspectives (7th and 10th grades). We predicted that 7th graders would be more willing to exclude others in the friendship and peer group contexts than would 4th graders, who are not focused on cliques yet, and 10th graders, who are past the peak of clique-oriented behavior. Given prior research which has shown that 7th and 10th graders have a more differentiated view of context than do 4th graders (Killen & Stangor, 2001), we predicted that younger children would be less likely to differentiate between the three contexts than would older children. We also predicted that 4th graders would be less likely than older children to differentiate between the gender and race targets given that racial stereotypes come later in childhood than do gender stereotypes. Further, we expected that 4th graders would be more persuaded by authority influences than would the 7th and 10th graders, and that adolescents would be more influenced by peer support for exclusion (social consensus) than would children of elementary school age. Based on prior findings about the importance of peer expectations (Horn, in press; Horn et al., 1999), we expected that, with age, children would view social consensus as increasingly significant, but only for the friendship and peer group contexts. For the school context, we expected that, with age, children and adolescents would view the social consensus from other citizens in the town as irrelevant to their own decision about exclusion from school based on group membership (for more on age-related hypotheses, see Goal 5, Chapter 2). Finally, given prior research findings that adolescents espouse a cultural relativity position in some contexts (Smetana, 1988), we expected that all 4th graders would judge it less permissible to exclude in other countries than would older children.

Regarding our hypotheses related to the gender of the participant, we predicted that females would judge it more wrong to exclude others than would males. This was based on our past studies, which have shown this to be a pervasive finding at different age periods (preschoolers: Killen et al., 2001; Theimer et al., 2001; elementary school: Killen et al., 2002; Killen & Stangor, 2001; adolescence: Horn, 2000; Killen et al., 2002; Killen & Stangor, 2001). Moreover, prior findings on prosocial development have also shown that females use more prosocial reasoning than do males (Eisenberg & Fabes, 1998; Wentzel & Erdley, 1993). Our interpretation about the gender findings has been that past experiences with exclusion (e.g., from sports or science-related activities) contribute to females' greater sensitivity to the wrongfulness of exclusion. However, we have not adequately tested this interpretation because we have not assessed individual participants' actual past history or their conceptualizations about their view of their own experience with exclusion. In addition, our interpretation has been limited by the fact that our prior studies sampled children solely from European-American backgrounds.

Another way to examine this issue would be to investigate whether males from minority ethnic groups that have traditionally experienced exclusion view exclusion as wrong to the same extent that females from nonminority backgrounds view exclusion. Thus, examining gender differences across and within children from different ethnic backgrounds will further understanding of the role of gender. On the one hand, we expected that gender differences would be minimal for the minority samples given that minority males have experienced exclusion in contrast to majority males who have not experienced exclusion based on race. On the other hand, African-American, Asian-American, and Latin-American cultures are more traditional in terms of gender roles than are the majority U.S. cultures (see Pessar, 1999; Rolandelli, 1991), indicating that minority males may be more willing then majority males to exclude a girl from a boys' club (or from friendship and school contexts). These conflicting messages led us to predict that minority males would look different from majority males but would be influenced by social pressure or indications that authority sanctioned the exclusion decision. Thus, we expected that gender differences would be more apparent in the European-American sample than in the minority samples. At the same time, it could be that gender differences would emerge for all four groups given that females have experienced exclusion and discrimination in a wide range of cultures.

We interviewed children and adolescents from four ethnic groups: European-American, African-American, Asian-American, and Latin-American. Given the predominance of Hispanic and Asian-American cultures in the United States, it is important to include children from these backgrounds in developmental research, particularly on topics such as exclusion from groups (Knight, Bernal, Cota, Garza, & Ocampo, 1993; Rumbaut & Portes, 2001).

Due to the low frequency of Asian-American and Latin-American participants, however, and given the demographics of the children in our schools, we combined these two groups into a third group, which we referred to as *Other Minority*. We recognize that there are significant differences between Asian-American and Latin-American cultural groups, but for the purposes of this study we combined them into one group. It was conceptually coherent to combine the two samples because these children had an "outsiders," perspective on the exclusion scenarios. Our interview protocol was about a White boy excluding a girl (gender target) or a Black child (race target). Thus, European-American and African-American children were the perpetrator and recipient of exclusion in the interview scenarios. The children in the Asian-American and Latin-American groups had a different perspective from the European-American and the African-American samples because they were not represented in the scenarios. In addition, the Asian-American and Latin-American participants in our study were from predominantly immigrant families, which have sociological, political, and historical experiences in the United States that are different from those of European-American or African-American children (see Fisher et al., 1998; Greenfield & Cocking, 1994; Ogbu, 1991; Pessar, 1999; Phinney, 1990; Rumbaut & Portes, 2001). Most important, our preliminary analyses revealed few significant differences between these two groups on their evaluations of exclusion (albeit the samples were small and this needs to be further investigated in a follow-up study).

We hypothesized that children who were not targets or perpetrators would evaluate acts of exclusion differently from children who matched the ethnicity of the protagonists in the scenarios. We predicted that minority children who were not the target of exclusion would evaluate exclusion as wrong, given their own past experience with exclusion as a minority member of U.S. culture. As immigrant cultures, many Latin-American and Asian-American children have family members who lived in another country, or they themselves were born in another country (Rumbaut & Portes, 2001). This family background may also dispose children from these cultures to a strong orientation toward the wrongfulness of exclusion. At the same time, children from Hispanic and Asian cultures may also be more willing to be influenced by authority given the more traditional and hierarchical aspects of these cultures (Greenfield & Cocking, 1994). This aspect of these immigrant cultures led us to predict that Asian and Hispanic children would judge exclusion as wrong but would be persuaded by the authority probe conditions to comply with the authority suggestion that exclusion is all right.

Further, we predicted that Asian and Hispanic children would be influenced by the generalizability assessment given their own family backgrounds. The generalizability probe asked participants whether the act of exclusion would be all right if it occurred in another country. We expected that Asian-American and Latin-American children in this study would be more willing to change their judgment on the basis of thinking about exclusion in another cultural setting. This is because the majority of these children have familiarity with a family member (or themselves) living in another country, which makes the issue very salient and personal for them. How it would influence children was an open question given the lack of prior research findings on this issue

37

Our general expectation was that children from all three minority backgrounds would use more fairness reasoning than would males from nonminority backgrounds due to the history of exclusion experienced by minority members in the United States. To assess these types of judgments, we generated a new justification category, referred to as *integration,* which reflected moral statements that went beyond the specific context of the interview (e.g., a friendship or peer club or school). Integration statements emphasize the moral necessity of inclusion for purposes of enabling people to treat each other with respect and equality. We expected that this category would be used by females and minority students more than by male nonminority students. All children in this study attended the same schools, which were mixed-ethnicity, middle-to lower-class socioeconomic status family backgrounds; thus all children had exposure and interaction with children from different ethnic backgrounds in the school setting.

III. METHOD

PARTICIPANTS

Participants included 294 students attending public schools in a suburban area of a large mid-Atlantic city. There were 84 fourth graders (M = 10.53 years, SD = 0.56, range 9.4 to 11.5 years) including 48 females and 36 males (26 European-American, 33 African-American, and 25 combined). There were 84 seventh graders (M = 13.72 years, SD = 0.56, range 12.0 to 14.9 years) including 43 females and 41 males (41 European-American, 21 African-American, and 22 combined), and 126 tenth graders (M = 16.27 years, SD = 0.80, range 14.5 to 18.3 years) including 73 females and 53 males (42 European-American, 42 African-American, and 42 combined). The ethnic breakdown of the sample was 37% European-American, 33% African-American, and 30% Latin-American and Asian-American combined (62% Latin-American, 38% Asian-American), fairly evenly divided by gender and age. The students were from primarily middle-class and working-class backgrounds as determined by the school district school records. All students were informed that the interviews were confidential, voluntary, and anonymous. Parental permission forms were distributed at school and all students who were given parental permission to participate were included in the study. All children attended schools with the same ethnic and socioeconomic backgrounds (mixed-ethnicity, middle- to working-class backgrounds).

PROCEDURE

A trained female research assistant interviewed children individually in a quiet room at school for approximately 25 minutes. For the majority of participants the race of the interviewer was matched with the race of the participant. Children were informed that the interviews were confidential and anonymous and that there were no right or wrong answers.

Stories were read to the participant, and cue cards ($8\frac{1}{2}''$ by $11''$) in large type of the story were placed in front of the participant in order to aid in comprehension and memory. The general format followed the structural-developmental interview method, which enables interviewers to probe children's reasoning ("Why?" or "How come?") while following a standard list of questions (for details on this interview methodology, see Damon, 1977; Kahn, 1999, Chap. 5; Turiel, 1983). All interviews were audiotaped and transcribed for analysis.

DESIGN

The interview consisted of six exclusion stories. There were three contexts of exclusion: friendship (excluding a potential friend), peer group (excluding someone from joining a music club), and school (excluding someone from attending school); there were two targets of exclusion: exclusion based on gender (female) and exclusion based on race (Black). Thus, for each of the three contexts there was a story of exclusion based on gender and a story of exclusion based on race. A within-subjects design was used; all children evaluated all six stories. (See Appendix A for the exact wording of scenarios used in the interviews and see Appendix B for a summary of the interview protocol design.)

Friendship Context

The friendship context involved a boy not wanting to be friends with a new neighbor because the new child is either a girl or is Black. Participants were first asked to *evaluate* the act of exclusion. For example, for the gender target, the participant was told that Tom does not want to be friends with Sally because she is a girl. The participant was asked if it was all right or not all right (*judgment*) for Tom not to be friends with Sally because she is a girl. The participant was also asked to provide a *justification* for his or her answer.

After the initial judgment of the exclusion, participants were asked three questions about external influences. The first question assessed the extent to which the participant would view *social consensus* as a legitimate reason to change the initial judgment of whether or not it is okay to exclude. For example, if the participant had judged exclusion in the friendship gender scenario as not okay, she was asked, "What if Tom's friends say that they don't think he should hang out with Sally because she's a girl. Would it be okay then to not hang out with her?" Conversely, if the participant had initially judged exclusion to be okay, she was asked, "What if Tom's friends say that they think Tom should hang out with Sally even though she's a girl. Would it be okay then for him not to hang out with her?" The source of social influence was also friends when the target of exclusion was race.

The second question involved the legitimacy of *authority influence* on determining whether or not exclusion is okay. If the participant judged exclusion as not all right—that is, it was not okay for Jerry to not hang out with Damon just because he is Black—then she was asked, "Would it make a difference if Jerry's parents said it was okay to not be friends with Damon?" Alternatively, if the participant evaluated the exclusion as all right, he was asked, "What if Jerry's parents say that it is not okay for him to not hang out with Damon because he's Black. Would it be okay then to not hang out with him?"

The third question examined the *generalizability* or cultural context of the situation. We tested whether the wrongfulness of exclusion applied only in the United States or whether it would be okay in another country for a boy to not be friends with someone because she's a girl or because he is Black. Participants were asked to provide justifications for their responses to all three probe questions.

Peer Group Context

The peer group context entailed a music club, either all boys or all White, whose members did not want to let a girl join or a Black child join because the club wanted to remain all boys or all White. The participant was told that the music club collected and traded music CDs, so that talent was not a factor in whether or not to include the individual. Participants were asked to evaluate exclusion (e.g., "Is it all right or not all right for Joe and his friends to not let Kevin join the club because he's Black?") and to provide justifications for their responses (see Appendix A for the exact wording).

For the first question about external influence, the source of influence was other students, social consensus influence, who wanted to join the music club. If the participant judged it to be not all right to exclude the Black child from the music club, he was asked, "What if other kids who want to join the club think that the club should not let Kevin join because he is Black. Would it be okay then to not let him join?" On the other hand, if the participant judged it to all right for the music club to exclude Kevin, he was asked, "What if other kids who want to join the club think that the club should let Kevin join even though he is Black. Would it be okay then to not let him join?"

In the authority influence question, the authority was the club leader's parents. For example after a judgment of *not okay* in the peer group–gender scenario, the participant was asked, "What if Mike's parents say that it's all right for the music club to not let Jessica join because she's a girl. Would it be okay then to not let Jessica join?" If the participant viewed exclusion as okay, she was asked, "What if Mike's parents say that the club should let Jessica join even though she's a girl. Would it be okay then to not let Jessica join?"

To determine whether or not the child evaluated exclusion from the peer group as universally okay or not okay, we asked participants to imagine the situation in another country. Participants were asked, "Would it be okay for a music club in another country to not let someone join because she is a girl or because someone is Black?" Participants were also asked to give justifications for their responses to all three external influence questions.

School Context

The school context involved a town that did not allow girls or did not allow Black children to go to school. Participants were asked if it was all right or not all right for the town to not allow girls or to not allow Black children to go to school. Participants were also asked to provide a justification for their answers.

For the social consensus question, the consensus referred to the people in the town. If the participant judged it to be not all right for the town to ban girls from going to school, she was asked, "What if the people in the town said that they don't think Amy should be allowed to go to school because she's a girl? Do you think it's okay, then?" Participants who evaluated the town's decision to forbid girls from going to school as acceptable were then asked, "What if the people in the town say that they think Amy should be allowed to go to school even though she's a girl? Do you think it's okay, then?"

For the authority influence question, the authority was the government. We asked participants who judged the town's decision as wrong to evaluate the legitimacy of the government to condone a town's decision to forbid girls or to forbid Black children from going to school. Likewise, if the participant judged the town's decision as all right, the question was whether it was still all right to exclude girls or Black children if the government said the town should let them attend school.

The generalizability question probed the extent to which participants judged excluding girls or Black children from school as similarly wrong in places outside of the United States. Participants were asked to provide justifications for their responses to all three external influence questions.

CODING

Coding Categories

As described above, children were asked to make two types of evaluations of exclusion in each context, referred to as judgments and justifications. Participants' judgment responses of *okay to exclude* received a 0 and responses of *not okay to exclude* received a 1 (as done in prior studies; see Nucci & Turiel, 1993; Killen et al., 2001; Killen & Smetana, 1999, for similar coding procedures). Justification responses were analyzed using a modification of the coding system for social reasoning used in previous research (Kahn, 1999; Killen et al., 2001; Killen & Stangor, 2001; Smetana, 1995; Theimer et al., 2001). The coding categories were *moral* (fairness, equality, rights, equal opportunity, empathy, integration, reduction of racism and sexism, and the wrongfulness of discrimination), *social-conventional* (social coordination, group functioning, group identity, social expectations, traditions, stereotypes, authority, government, and social consensus), and *psychological* (personal choice). See Table 1 for the justification category descriptions.

Reliability Coding

Reliability coding was calculated on the justification data and was calculated using 37 percent of the interviews (1,704 data points). Using Cohen's kappa, inter-rater agreement in scoring the overall responses was .903 (percentage agreement = 94.5). Reliability was also calculated by justification coding category (moral, social-conventional, personal, and uncodable; see Table 1 for category descriptions); using Cohen's kappa, inter-rater agreement was .932 (percentage agreement = 96.7).

Stability of Judgment Variable (Change)

In order to conduct analyses on the stability of children's exclusion judgments, we created *change* variables. These variables reflected children's change (or absence of change) on their judgments after hearing the exclusion question (e.g., "Do you think it's okay for Tom to not hang out with Sally because she is a girl?") for each of the external influence probes: social consensus (e.g., "What if Tom's friends don't think he should hang out with Sally because she's a girl?"), authority influence (e.g., "What if Tom's parents say it's okay for Tom to not hang out with Sally because she's a girl?"), and generalizability (e.g., "Would it be okay in another country for a boy not to hang out with someone because she's a girl?"). Each of the change variables reflected the proportion of students who changed their judgments from not okay to exclude to okay to exclude or from okay to exclude to not okay to exclude. If children did not change their exclusion judgment, then they were assigned a 0; if children changed their judgment, they were assigned a 1 (*no change* = 0; *change* = 1). Then analyses were conducted on the proportion of children who changed from okay to exclude to not okay to exclude (or the other direction). Changing from okay to not okay was referred to as the *positive direction* (toward rejecting exclusion) and changing from not okay to okay was referred to as the *negative direction* (toward supporting exclusion).

STORY ORDER

Story order was counterbalanced within gender and race stories. Stories involving targets based on gender (gender stories) were presented before stories involving targets based on race (race stories) due to pilot work which indicated that participants are more likely to support gender exclusion than exclusion based on race. Friendship, peer group, and school contexts were counterbalanced; there were no significant story order effects.

IV. RESULTS

OVERVIEW AND PLAN FOR ANALYSIS

We present analyses of the judgments and justifications used in the evaluation of exclusion (Question 1 in Appendix A) for each of three contexts (friendship, peer group, and school) and for each target group (gender and race). First, we describe the overall findings regarding comparisons of the three contexts across both target groups, and regarding comparisons of the target groups across the three contexts. Then we describe the results that are specific to particular scenarios, as well as those specifically related to the participant variables, including the gender, ethnicity, and grade of the participant. Second, analyses of the three *external influence probes*: social consensus, authority influence, and generalizability of exclusion (Questions 3, 5, and 7, respectively, in Appendix A), are reported. Third, analyses of the *change assessment*, which reflects participants' change in judgment responses from *okay to exclude* to *not okay to exclude* (and vice versa), are described.

The term *scenario* is used to indicate a particular context and target combination, such as friendship–race. Reference to a particular *context* refers to that context across both target groups. For example, the school context is a composite of the school gender and the school race scenarios (the average of the two scenarios). Composites were also made across contexts for each *target* group. *Gender target* refers to the collapsed categories of friendship–gender, peer group–gender, and school–gender. *Race target* refers to the collapsed categories of friendship–race, peer group–race, and school–race.

Judgments were coded dichotomously (0 = *okay to exclude*, 1 = *not okay to exclude*), and justifications were the proportions of fairness, empathy, integration, group functioning, social tradition, authority, social influence, and personal choice categories (see Table 1). For justification analyses, we first conducted tests on the categories used most often across all contexts (using a criteria of .10 frequency or higher). Then we conducted analyses on all eight justification categories to test specific hypotheses about each of the justifications for each scenario.

For judgment analyses, we first tested the overall design for context and target main effects using $2 \times 3 \times 3 \times 3 \times 2$ (Gender of Participant: female, male × Grade of Participant: 4th, 7th, 10th × Ethnicity of Participant: European-American, African-American, Other Minority × Context of Exclusion: friendship, peer group, school × Target of Exclusion: gender, race) MANOVAs with repeated measures on the last two factors for each question separately. Post hoc comparisons were performed using Tukey's HSD, and $2 \times 3 \times 3$ (Gender of Participant × Grade of Participant × Ethnicity of Participant) ANOVAs were conducted to test for between-subject effects. In cases where the assumption of sphericity was not met in multivariate analyses, corrections were made using the Huynh-Feldt method.

For justification analyses, we conducted tests using the four predominant justification categories to provide an overall picture of the pattern of results to match the report of the findings for judgments. In addition, we conducted $2 \times 3 \times 3 \times 8$ (Gender of Participant × Grade of Participant × Ethnicity of Participant × Justification: fairness, empathy, integration, group functioning, social tradition, authority, social influence, personal choice) ANOVAs with repeated measures on the last factor for each scenario.

OVERALL FINDINGS

How Do Children Evaluate Exclusion?

Do Judgments of Exclusion Vary by the Context?

It was hypothesized that context, regardless of whether the target of exclusion was a girl or a Black child, would make a difference in the way children and adolescents evaluate exclusion of an individual. Analyses confirmed a main effect for context, $F(2, 552) = 56.47$, $p < .001$, indicating that children and adolescents were more likely to judge exclusion from school ($M = .98$, $SD = .10$) as not okay than to judge exclusion from friendship ($M = .78$, $SD = .33$) or from the peer group ($M = .79$, $SD = .31$) as wrong, $p < .001$.

Do Judgments of Exclusion Vary by the Target?

Analysis of the full design revealed that participants also differentiated between the target groups when evaluating exclusion, $F(1, 276) = 58.25$, $p < .001$. As predicted, across contexts, exclusion based on race ($M = .91$, $SD = .20$) was more likely to be judged as not okay than was exclusion based on gender ($M = .79$, $SD = .24$).

46

Do Judgments for Gender and Race Targets Vary by the Context of Exclusion?

A Context × Target interaction, $F(1.85, 552) = 15.17$, $p < .001$, indicated that although overall context and overall target effects were significant, there were also differences between particular scenarios. Further analyses revealed that for the friendship context and the peer group context, the main effect for target held; exclusion of a Black child was more likely to be viewed as wrong than was exclusion of a girl. However, no differentiation in the wrongfulness of exclusion was made between excluding a girl and excluding a Black child from school; both scenarios were viewed as not okay by the vast majority of participants (for all means, see Table 2).

Are There Gender, Grade, or Ethnicity Differences for Exclusion Judgments?

Based on our hypotheses about the importance of developmental changes and experiential factors to an individual's evaluation and reasoning about exclusion, we were interested in the effect of between-subjects factors (gender, grade, and ethnicity) on judgments. In the repeated measures MANOVA that tested the full design, an overall grade (age) effect

TABLE 2

PROPORTION OF NEGATIVE JUDGMENTS ABOUT EXCLUSION

	Friendship Context				Peer Group Context				School Context			
	Gender		Race		Gender		Race		Gender		Race	
	M	SD	M	SD	M	SD	M	SD	M	SD	M	SD
Grade 4												
Female	.75	(.44)	.88	(.33)	.81	(.39)	.90	(.31)	1.0	(.00)	1.0	(.00)
Male	.75	(.44)	.92	(.28)	.78	(.42)	.92	(.28)	1.0	(.00)	1.0	(.00)
Total	.75	(.44)	.89	(.31)	.80	(.40)	.90	(.30)	1.0	(.00)	1.0	(.00)
Grade 7												
Female	.72	(.45)	.93	(.26)	.84	(.37)	.95	(.21)	.98	(.15)	1.0	(.00)
Male	.78	(.42)	.90	(.30)	.68	(.47)	.95	(.22)	.98	(.16)	.98	(.16)
Total	.75	(.44)	.92	(.28)	.76	(.43)	.95	(.21)	.98	(.15)	.99	(.11)
Grade 10												
Female	.67	(.47)	.85	(.36)	.60	(.49)	.86	(.35)	1.0	(.00)	.97	(.16)
Male	.55	(.50)	.75	(.43)	.58	(.50)	.79	(.41)	.94	(.23)	.98	(.14)
Total	.62	(.49)	.81	(.39)	.60	(.49)	.83	(.37)	.98	(.15)	.98	(.15)
Total	.69	(.46)	.86	(.34)	.70	(.46)	.89	(.32)	.98	(.13)	.99	(.12)

Note.—$N = 294$. Proportions cannot exceed 1.00. Standard deviations are in parentheses.

was found, $F(2, 276) = 9.99$, $p < .001$. Across all scenarios, 10th graders ($M = .80$, $SD = .20$) were more likely than 4th graders ($M = .89$, $SD = .15$) or 7th graders ($M = .89$, $SD = .15$) to evaluate exclusion as okay, $ps < .001$. A Context × Grade interaction, $F(4, 552) = 3.03$, $p < .017$, revealed that 10th graders ($Ms = .71$, $SDs = 0.37, 0.32$, for friendship and peer group, respectively) were more likely than 4th graders ($Ms = .82, .85$, $SDs = .28$, $.27$, friendship and peer group, respectively) or 7th graders ($Ms = .83$, $.86$, $SDs = .30, .24$, friendship and peer group, respectively) to evaluate the friendship and peer group contexts as legitimate situations for exclusion, $ps < .048$ (range = .002 to .048). In other words, 10th graders were more likely than 4th graders or 7th graders to judge exclusion from friendship or from peer group as okay, regardless of whether the individual being excluded was a girl or a Black child. Judgments of exclusion in the school context, however, did not differ across grades.

When between-subjects effects were analyzed using univariate ANOVAs, grade effects were found for the peer group–gender scenario, $F(2, 276) = 5.57$, $p < .004$, and for the peer group–race scenario, $F(2, 276) = 2.92$, $p < .022$. As shown in Table 2, 10th graders were more likely to view excluding a girl from an all-boys music club as okay than were 4th graders, $p < .005$ and 7th graders, $p < .025$. Likewise, 10th graders were more likely than 7th graders to judge not allowing a Black child to join an all-White music club as okay, $p < .021$. Although grade effects for both friendship–gender, $F(2, 276) = 3.59$, $p < .029$, and friendship–race, $F(2, 276) = 2.92$, $p < .022$, scenarios were indicated, post hoc comparisons revealed no significant grade differences for either scenario.

Summary

When evaluating whether it was okay or not okay to exclude someone, children and adolescents differentiated between the contexts of exclusion and between the targets of exclusion. School was not a legitimate context for exclusion; however, some children and adolescents viewed friendship and peer group contexts as situations in which exclusion may be justifiable. Furthermore, excluding a girl from friendship or from the peer group was more okay than excluding a Black child in those contexts. From 7th to 10th grade, exclusion was evaluated less negatively, particularly in the peer group context.

What Types of Reasons Do Children Give for Their Judgments About Exclusion?

Four of the eight justification categories (fairness, empathy, group functioning, and personal choice) were used most often by children and adolescents to reason about exclusion of a girl or a Black child from friendship, peer group, and school contexts. For an overview of justifications, these four were analyzed, given that they were tied to our hypotheses and occurred with a frequency greater than .10. In addition, we conducted analyses on all eight categories for a closer examination of justifications for each scenario.

Do Reasons About Exclusion Vary by the Context?

It was hypothesized that context would make a difference in the way children and adolescents reasoned about the exclusion of an individual, regardless of whether the target of exclusion was a girl or a Black child. As shown in Table 3, in which we report justification proportions collapsed for target and displayed for the three contexts, results confirmed our expectations that justifications would vary by context. Participants used the fairness justification predominately across all contexts; however, it was used the most for the school context, $p < .001$. Empathy and personal choice justifications were used primarily for the friendship context, $p < .001$, and group functioning was used only for the peer group context, $p < .001$.

A 4th-grade African-American girl used fairness justification for the friendship context:

> I don't think it's fair because you can't just have boy friends, you have to have some girls that are your friends, and he shouldn't judge her by if it's a boy or a girl, he should judge them by personality and stuff . . . like if they are a meanie or like you give them something and they won't give it back or share.

In contrast, a 7th-grade European-American boy, who evaluated the decision of a boy who did not want to be friends with a girl, used personal choice reasoning:

> I think it's okay because boys and girls don't get that much along. Right now, it's like Tom should make his decision about who he wants to hang out with. You pick your friends. It's something you do on your own. It's really up to you to decide.

Do Reasons About Exclusion Vary by the Target?

Justifications also varied by the target. As shown in Table 4, in which we report justification proportions collapsed for context and displayed

49

TABLE 3
PROPORTIONS OF JUSTIFICATIONS BY CONTEXT

	Assessment by Context																							
	Exclusion						Social Consensus						Authority						Generalizability					
	Friend		Peer		School		Friend		Peer		School		Friend		Peer		School		Friend		Peer		School	
Justification	M	(SD)	M	(SD)	M	(SD)	M	(SD)	M	(SD)	M	(SD)	M	(SD)	M	(SD)	M	(SD)	M	(SD)	M	(SD)	M	(SD)
Fairness	.65	(.35)	.63	(.33)	.96	(.15)	.33	(.35)	.48	(.37)	.88	(.26)	.41	(.38)	.47	(.26)	.81	(.33)	.53	(.38)	.59	(.37)	.84	(.29)
Empathy	.07	(.18)	.06	(.32)	.00	(.06)	.04	(.13)	.05	(.15)	.02	(.09)	.05	(.16)	.03	(.12)	.02	(.10)	.05	(.15)	.03	(.12)	.01	(.07)
Integration	.04	(.16)	.02	(.12)	.01	(.09)	.01	(.09)	.01	(.08)	.01	(.09)	.02	(.11)	.03	(.12)	.01	(.08)	.03	(.12)	.03	(.14)	.01	(.09)
Group functioning	.00	(.03)	.25	(.29)	.00	(.00)	.00	(.00)	.36	(.37)	.00	(.02)	.00	(.00)	.26	(.33)	.00	(.03)	.00	(.01)	.14	(.26)	.00	(.03)
Social tradition	.02	(.10)	.04	(.14)	.01	(.08)	.00	(.04)	.00	(.06)	.00	(.04)	.00	(.04)	.01	(.07)	.00	(.03)	.12	(.23)	.13	(.26)	.07	(.20)
Authority	.00	(.03)	.00	(.00)	.00	(.04)	.01	(.08)	.00	(.00)	.01	(.08)	.14	(.26)	.14	(.30)	.12	(.27)	.01	(.09)	.02	(.09)	.02	(.10)
Social influence	.00	(.06)	.00	(.01)	.00	(.03)	.02	(.12)	.04	(.14)	.02	(.12)	.00	(.00)	.00	(.00)	.00	(.00)	.00	(.03)	.00	(.00)	.00	(.04)
Personal choice	.20	(.31)	.03	(.03)	.00	(.01)	.53	(.38)	.02	(.11)	.02	(.10)	.33	(.36)	.03	(.12)	.00	(.03)	.20	(.31)	.00	(.04)	.00	(.03)

Note.—N = 294. Proportions cannot exceed 1.0. Standard deviations in parentheses. Friend = friendship context, Peer = peer group context, School = school context.

TABLE 4

PROPORTIONS OF JUSTIFICATIONS BY TARGET

	Assessment by Target															
	Exclusion				Social Consensus				Authority				Generalizability			
	Gender		Race		Gender		Race		Gender		Race		Gender		Race	
Justification	M	SD	M	SD	M	SD	M	SD	M	SD	M	SD	M	SD	M	SD
Fairness	.68	(.25)	.82	(.23)	.50	(.25)	.62	(.29)	.49	(.30)	.63	(.33)	.57	(.30)	.74	(.29)
Empathy	.05	(.13)	.04	(.21)	.04	(.12)	.03	(.12)	.03	(.10)	.03	(.12)	.03	(.09)	.03	(.12)
Integration	.02	(.08)	.04	(.12)	.01	(.06)	.02	(.08)	.01	(.07)	.03	(.12)	.01	(.07)	.04	(.11)
Group functioning	.11	(.15)	.06	(.11)	.14	(.16)	.11	(.17)	.11	(.15)	.06	(.13)	.07	(.13)	.03	(.09)
Social tradition	.04	(.10)	.01	(.07)	.00	(.05)	.00	(.04)	.00	(.04)	.00	(.05)	.16	(.25)	.06	(.16)
Authority	.00	(.03)	.00	(.02)	.00	(.04)	.00	(.04)	.18	(.29)	.09	(.20)	.01	(.07)	.02	(.11)
Social influence	.00	(.03)	.00	(.04)	.05	(.15)	.02	(.02)	.00	(.00)	.00	(.00)	.00	(.03)	.00	(.02)
Personal choice	.09	(.15)	.04	(.11)	.21	(.16)	.17	(.19)	.18	(.29)	.10	(.16)	.10	(.15)	.04	(.11)

Note.—N = 294. Proportions cannot exceed 1.0. Standard deviations in parentheses.

for the two targets, fairness was used more for exclusion of the race target than for the gender target, $p < .001$, whereas empathy, group functioning, and personal choice were used more often for the gender target than for the race target. Thus, children and adolescents used more nonmoral justifications for gender than for race, indicating a belief that exclusion based on gender is sometimes justified as necessary for group functioning or for personal choice, but is not a matter of right or wrong.

Do Reasons for Gender and Race Targets Vary by the Context of Exclusion?

It was also hypothesized that children and adolescents would differ in their reasoning about excluding a girl or a Black child for particular scenarios. As expected, participants viewed exclusion of a Black child as more wrong than exclusion of a girl. For both friendship and peer group contexts, fairness was used more to reason about the exclusion of a Black child than about the exclusion of a girl. However, for the school context, a vast majority of participants viewed exclusion as equally unfair for both scenarios. For example, a 4th-grade European-American boy used fairness to reason about excluding a girl from school, "It's not all right because it's not like girls have this certain disease. There is no difference between anybody and everybody should be able to go to school." When asked about excluding an African-American child from school, a 10th-grade African-American girl replied, "It's an educational matter and you should have freedom of education no matter what color you turn out to be. You are still a person, same organs, maybe the skin stuff is a little different but that shouldn't have anything to do with it."

In contrast, nonmoral justifications were used more for reasoning about the exclusion of a girl and were limited to certain contexts. Group functioning justification was primarily used for the peer group context, with higher use for the exclusion of a girl than of a Black child. Likewise, personal choice was limited to one context, friendship, and used more to reason about the exclusion of a girl than of a Black child (for all means, see Table 5).

A 10th-grade male emphasized the idea that being friends with someone is a personal choice in the friendship–gender scenario: "I think it's up to him even though I don't think it's very nice for him to not hang out with Sally just because she's a girl. But I do think it's his choice."

A 4th-grade European-American boy focused on group functioning when reasoning about the peer group–gender scenario:

> It's okay because it's their club and they put the whole thing together and they can do what they want at their club. It would be nicer if they let the girl in but they designed it and they did everything and that's how it will work.

TABLE 5

PROPORTIONS OF JUSTIFICATIONS BY SCENARIO

Assessment by Justification	Scenario											
	Friendship Context				Peer Group Context				School Context			
	Gender		Race		Gender		Race		Gender		Race	
	M	SD	M	SD	M	SD	M	SD	M	SD	M	SD
Exclusion												
Fairness	.55	(.49)	.75	(.42)	.53	(.47)	.74	(.40)	.95	(.20)	.96	(.20)
Empathy	.09	(.28)	.05	(.19)	.06	(.22)	.06	(.60)	.01	(.10)	.01	(.05)
Integration	.03	(.16)	.06	(.23)	.01	(.10)	.04	(.19)	.01	(.08)	.02	(.14)
Group functioning	.00	(.06)	.00	(.03)	.33	(.44)	.17	(.33)	.00	(.00)	.00	(.00)
Social tradition	.03	(.17)	.01	(.10)	.07	(.24)	.02	(.13)	.01	(.11)	.01	(.09)
Authority	.00	(.06)	.00	(.00)	.00	(.00)	.00	(.00)	.01	(.07)	.00	(.06)
Social influence	.01	(.08)	.01	(.08)	.00	(.00)	.00	(.03)	.00	(.00)	.01	(.07)
Personal choice	.27	(.44)	.13	(.32)	.00	(.00)	.01	(.07)	.00	(.03)	.00	(.00)
Social consensus												
Fairness	.22	(.40)	.45	(.48)	.40	(.47)	.55	(.48)	.88	(.32)	.87	(.33)
Empathy	.05	(.20)	.03	(.16)	.05	(.21)	.04	(.18)	.01	(.11)	.03	(.15)
Integration	.01	(.10)	.01	(.08)	.01	(.12)	.02	(.13)	.01	(.08)	.03	(.16)
Group functioning	.00	(.00)	.00	(.00)	.41	(.47)	.31	(.52)	.00	(.03)	.00	(.03)
Social tradition	.00	(.06)	.01	(.09)	.01	(.09)	.01	(.07)	.01	(.08)	.00	(.03)
Authority	.00	(.06)	.00	(.06)	.00	(.00)	.00	(.00)	.01	(.12)	.01	(.10)
Social influence	.08	(.26)	.03	(.17)	.06	(.23)	.02	(.13)	.02	(.15)	.02	(.15)
Personal choice	.62	(.47)	.44	(.48)	.01	(.09)	.04	(.19)	.02	(.12)	.02	(.12)
Authority influence												
Fairness	.29	(.45)	.53	(.48)	.36	(.47)	.58	(.48)	.81	(.38)	.80	(.40)
Empathy	.05	(.21)	.05	(.21)	.02	(.15)	.04	(.18)	.02	(.12)	.02	(.12)
Integration	.02	(.14)	.03	(.16)	.01	(.12)	.05	(.21)	.01	(.08)	.02	(.14)
Group functioning	.00	(.00)	.00	(.00)	.34	(.46)	.19	(.38)	.00	(.00)	.00	(.06)
Social tradition	.00	(.00)	.01	(.09)	.01	(.12)	.01	(.09)	.00	(.00)	.01	(.07)
Authority	.20	(.40)	.08	(.26)	.22	(.52)	.07	(.25)	.14	(.34)	.12	(.31)
Social influence	.00	(.00)	.00	(.00)	.00	(.00)	.00	(.00)	.00	(.00)	.00	(.00)
Personal choice	.39	(.48)	.27	(.43)	.02	(.13)	.05	(.20)	.01	(.07)	.00	(.00)
Generalizability												
Fairness	.40	(.48)	.66	(.47)	.48	(.49)	.70	(.45)	.82	(.37)	.86	(.34)
Empathy	.04	(.17)	.06	(.22)	.03	(.17)	.03	(.17)	.01	(.08)	.01	(.10)
Integration	.02	(.13)	.04	(.20)	.01	(.12)	.06	(.23)	.01	(.10)	.02	(.13)
Group functioning	.00	(.00)	.00	(.03)	.21	(.40)	.08	(.26)	.00	(.00)	.00	(.06)
Social tradition	.18	(.37)	.06	(.22)	.19	(.39)	.07	(.26)	.11	(.31)	.04	(.20)
Authority	.01	(.11)	.01	(.11)	.01	(.07)	.03	(.16)	.02	(.12)	.02	(.14)
Social influence	.00	(.06)	.00	(.00)	.00	(.00)	.00	(.00)	.00	(.06)	.00	(.06)
Personal choice	.28	(.44)	.13	(.33)	.01	(.07)	.00	(.03)	.00	(.06)	.00	(.03)

Note.—N = 294. Proportions cannot exceed 1.00. Standard deviations are in parentheses.

They know what they want to do. She could make her own club and do exactly the same thing with girls.

When reasoning about exclusion in the peer group–race scenario, a 10th-grade African-American female used a fairness justification:

That's messed up. Joe has the club and it's all White people and they don't want to let him in, that's messed up, period. He's supposed to be our friend but yet he's not letting you in because of that; it's just not fair. If you want to get along in the world you've going to have to know certain things, like some people think, being Black, they don't want to hang out with them because of that, but it's just wrong, period.

Are There Gender, Grade, or Ethnicity Differences for Reasoning About Exclusion?

As predicted, children's and adolescents' reasoning about exclusion varied depending on their gender, grade, or ethnicity. A Justification × Grade × Ethnicity × Gender interaction, $F(28, 1932) = 1.619$, $p < .02$, showed that for the friendship–gender scenario, 10th-grade European-American boys ($M = .31$, $SD = .46$) used less fairness reasoning than did 10th-grade Other Minority boys ($M = .68$, $SD = .48$), $p < .05$. In addition, 7th-grade European-American boys ($M = .74$, $SD = .45$) used more fairness reasoning than did 10th-grade European-American boys ($M = .31$, $SD = .46$), $p < .05$. For the friendship–race context, both grade, $F(14, 1932) = 2.54$, $p < .01$, and ethnicity, $F(14, 1932) = 4.61$, $p < .001$, effects were found. Seventh graders ($M = .84$, $SD = .36$) were more likely to use fairness reasoning than were 4th graders ($M = .68$, $SD = .45$), and African-American children ($M = .63$, $SD = .46$) were less likely to use fairness to reason about exclusion than were European-American children ($M = .82$, $SD = .36$) or Other Minority children ($M = 0.79$, $SD = 0.40$), $p < .01$.

A close examination of why African-American children used the category of fairness less than the other children revealed that integration justification was used more often by African-American children ($M = 0.12$, $SD = 0.32$) than by European-Americans ($M = 0.02$, $SD = 0.13$) or Other Minority children ($M = 0.03$, $SD = 0.18$), $p < .05$. In other words, for the friendship–race scenario, compared to other ethnicities, African-American children used both fairness and integration to evaluate why it was not okay for a Black child to be excluded from being friends with a White child (integration included the use of fairness and rights). As an illustration of the use of integration, a 10th-grade African-American girl shared her insights about the consequences of a boy to not wanting to be friends with someone because of skin color:

It's not okay ... Because he's going to see everybody. He's gonna see Black people, he's gonna see White people, he's gonna see Asian people, he's going to see Cambodians, he's gonna see Ethiopians. I mean, yes, people do come from different places, and yes, they do speak different languages. But everybody has a heart, and they also have feelings, and they also know how it is to be put down. And it hurts. So I mean if you're the type of person who says, "Okay, I don't like you because of a reason like that," it is just wrong.

Analyses of empathy revealed that, although used less frequently than other categories, when empathy reasoning was used, there were grade, gender, and ethnicity effects. An overall between-subjects grade effect was found, $F(2, 276) = 3.25$, $p < .04$, indicating that across all scenarios the use of empathy decreased with age. Fourth graders ($M = .08$, $SD = .14$), compared to 10th graders ($M = .02$, $SD = .15$), used more empathy to reason about exclusion. This was especially true for the friendship–gender scenario, as follow-up analyses indicated 4th graders ($M = .17$, $SD = .37$) used more empathy reasoning than did 10th graders ($M = .04$, $SD = .19$), $p < .01$. In addition, an overall between-subjects ethnicity effect was found, $F(2, 276) = 4.99$, $p < .01$. African-American children ($M = .07$, $SD = .20$) used more empathy reasoning to evaluate exclusion than did European-American children ($M = .02$, $SD = .06$), $p < .01$. Follow-up analyses revealed that 4th-grade African-American boys ($M = .40$, $SD = .51$) were more likely to use empathy reasoning than were 4th-grade African-American girls ($M = .06$, $SD = .16$), $p < .01$, 4th-grade European-American boys ($M = .00$, $SD = .00$), $p < .02$, or 10th-grade African-American boys ($M = .06$, $SD = .25$), $p < .03$. In addition, an ethnicity effect, $F(14, 1932) = 4.611$, $p < .00$, was found for the friendship–race scenario. African-Americans ($M = .11$, $SD = .29$) viewed exclusion in terms of empathy more than did European-Americans ($M = .01$, $SD = .08$) or Other Minority children ($M = .02$, $SD = .12$), $p < .01$.

As an example of empathy reasoning in an exclusion scenario, a 4th-grade African-American boy said, "It's not ok because they are not letting him. ... It's like really upsetting that he can't make new friends and he just moved in. It's probably really sad."

A 10th-grade African-American male used a combination of empathy and fairness when justifying why it is wrong to not be friends with someone because of race: "Because if that would of happened to him, he would feel sorry just like Damon because Damon wants to play with him and it's not fair that Jerry doesn't want to hang out with him."

As predicted, the use of group functioning increased with age, as indicted by an overall between-subjects grade effect, $F(2, 276) = 4.68$, $p < .01$. Tenth graders ($M = .10$, $SD = .10$) viewed exclusion more in terms of group functioning than did 7th graders ($M = .06$, $SD = .08$), $p < .01$. A closer examination of individual scenarios revealed significant use of group functioning reasoning for the peer group–gender scenario. Tenth graders ($M = .42$, $SD = .46$) more often used group functioning to reason about the exclusion of a girl from an all-boys music club than did 4th graders ($M = .29$, $SD = .43$), $p < .001$. In addition, an overall gender effect, $F(1, 276) = 8.11$, $p < .01$, indicated that, when reasoning about exclusion, boys ($M = .11$, $SD = .10$) were more likely to use group functioning reasoning than were girls ($M = .07$, $SD = .09$), $p < .01$. Again, follow-up analyses indicated that this was significant for the peer group–gender scenario. Boys ($M = .42$, $SD = .46$) viewed exclusion in terms of group functioning more than did girls ($M = .26$, $SD = .42$), $p < .001$.

A 7th-grade European-American boy viewed exclusion of a girl from the music club in terms of group functioning:

> I think that Mike and his friends are right for not letting her in the club because it's their club and then like if they don't want girls to join and make it an all-boys club that's okay. They like the same kind of music. If she wanted to make her own group then she can do it and make it so that no boys are allowed.

A 7th-grade European-American girl, however, viewed this type of exclusion quite differently. She said the following about an all-boys club's decision to exclude a girl:

> In a way, yes, and in a way, no, because it's trying to keep her out just because she's a girl. That's discrimination. But boys, they talk about stuff, that you know, girls just don't like or don't like doing. But really, they don't have a good reason not to let her in and I think it's a form of discrimination.

Finally, the use of personal choice increased with age across all scenarios, as shown by an overall grade effect, $F(2, 276) = 7.29$, $p < .001$. Tenth graders ($M = .09$, $SD = .12$) evaluated exclusion using personal choice reasons more than did 4th graders or 7th graders ($Ms = .05$, $SDs = .09$), $p < .05$. Follow-up analyses indicated that this was significant for the friendship–gender scenario. Tenth graders ($M = .37$, $SD = .48$) were more likely to view exclusion of a girl from being friends with a boy as a personal choice issue than were 4th graders ($M = .20$, $SD = .40$), $p < .02$.

Summary

In sum, as hypothesized, children's and adolescents' reasoning about exclusion of a girl or a Black child from friendship, peer group, and school contexts varied depending on context, target, and participant variables. Overall, when fairness was used to reject exclusion, it was used by a majority of individuals across all contexts and targets. However, there was significant variation among participants for the friendship–gender and friendship–race scenarios, as grade, ethnicity, and gender differences were found. One of the most significant findings was that African-Americans, compared to other ethnicities, used more integration reasoning to justify why a Black child should not be excluded from being friends with a White child. This means that they went beyond the scenario and discussed the wrongfulness and unfairness of exclusion in the larger context of society by elaborating on the negative consequences of discrimination. Although not used with great frequency, empathy was used more often by younger children to reason about exclusion than by older children. African-American 4th-grade males were the most likely group to use empathy. Finally, the use of nonmoral justifications, group functioning and personal choice, increased with age. Older children were more likely to view exclusion of a girl from being friends with a boy as a personal issue, and exclusion of a girl from an all-boys music club as a group functioning issue. In addition, boys used more group functioning justification than did girls.

EXTERNAL INFLUENCE PROBES

How Does Social Consensus Influence Children's Judgments of Exclusion?

Do Judgments Regarding Social Consensus Vary by the Context of Exclusion?

We were interested in how children and adolescents evaluated exclusion after they heard counterprobes of others' opinions that exclusion was either okay or not okay (see Appendix B for the design). A main effect for context was found, $F(2, 550) = 32.39$, $p < .001$, indicating that participants evaluated exclusion in the three contexts differently after hearing that others held an opposing viewpoint about exclusion. The friendship context ($M = .79$, $SD = .32$) was more likely to elicit judgments of okay than was either the peer group context ($M = .85$, $SD = .28$) or the school context ($M = .97$, $SD = .14$), $ps < .005$. Moreover, the school context was viewed as the least legitimate forum for exclusion, $ps < .001$.

Do Judgments Regarding Social Consensus Vary by the Target of Exclusion?

As for the analyses of the initial evaluation of exclusion, a main effect for the target of exclusion was significant for the social consensus question, $F(1, 275) = 32.32$, $p < .001$. Without taking context into effect, the gender target ($M = .82$, $SD = .23$) was more likely to be judged as okay to exclude than was the race target ($M = .92$, $SD = .19$).

Do Judgments Regarding Social Consensus for Gender and Race Targets Vary by the Context of Exclusion?

The main effects for context and target were qualified by a Context × Target interaction, $F(1.89, 550) = 9.14$, $p < .001$. The friendship and peer group contexts were differentiated when controlling for the target group, but further analyses revealed that this was not the case when comparing the three contexts for each target group separately. In other words, reasoning about friendship–gender and peer group–gender did not differ, but both differed from school–gender, $ps < .001$. Likewise, friendship–race and peer group–race differed from school–race, $p < .001$, but not from each other. The main effect for target, which indicated that exclusion based on gender was more likely to be viewed as okay than was exclusion based on race, was also qualified by the finding that judgments did not differ between school–gender and school–race (see Table 6 for all means).

TABLE 6

PROPORTION OF NEGATIVE JUDGMENTS FOR SOCIAL CONSENSUS

	Friendship Context				Peer Group Context				School Context			
	Gender		Race		Gender		Race		Gender		Race	
	M	SD	M	SD	M	SD	M	SD	M	SD	M	SD
Grade 4												
Female	.71	(.46)	.90	(.31)	.92	(.28)	.92	(.28)	.94	(.24)	.96	(.20)
Male	.81	(.40)	.89	(.32)	.83	(.38)	.92	(.28)	.97	(.17)	.94	(.23)
Total	.75	(.44)	.89	(.31)	.88	(.33)	.92	(.28)	.95	(.21)	.95	(.21)
Grade 7												
Female	.86	(.35)	.93	(.26)	.88	(.32)	.95	(.21)	.95	(.22)	1.0	(.00)
Male	.66	(.48)	.93	(.26)	.78	(.42)	.95	(.22)	.98	(.16)	.93	(.26)
Total	.76	(.43)	.93	(.26)	.83	(.37)	.95	(.21)	.96	(.19)	.96	(.19)
Grade 10												
Female	.71	(.46)	.85	(.36)	.74	(.44)	.92	(.28)	.96	(.19)	.99	(.12)
Male	.62	(.49)	.75	(.43)	.66	(.48)	.81	(.40)	.98	(.14)	1.0	(.00)
Total	.67	(.47)	.81	(.39)	.71	(.46)	.87	(.33)	.97	(.18)	.99	(.09)
Total	.72	(.45)	.87	(.34)	.79	(.41)	.91	(.29)	.96	(.19)	.97	(.16)

Note.—$N = 294$. Proportions cannot exceed 1.00. Standard deviations are in parentheses.

Are There Gender, Grade, or Ethnicity Differences for Judgments Regarding Social Consensus?

Tests for overall between-subjects effects revealed that, across all scenarios, 10th graders ($M = .84$, $SD = .19$) were more likely than 7th graders ($M = .90$, $SD = .15$) to evaluate exclusion as okay, $F(2, 275) = 5.94$, $p < .003$, after hearing the social consensus probe. A Context × Grade interaction, $F(4, 550) = 3.91$, $p < .004$, illustrated that grade differences were significant for the friendship context, $F(2, 291) = 3.11$, $p < .046$, and the peer group context, $F(2, 291) = 5.47$, $p < .005$, but not for the school context. For both the friendship context and the peer group context, 10th graders ($Ms = .74$, $.79$, $SDs = .36$, $.32$, for friendship and peer group, respectively) were more likely to view exclusion as okay than were 7th graders ($Ms = .85$, $.89$, $SDs = .28$, $.22$, $ps < .054$, $.020$, for friendship and peer group, respectively). In addition, 10th graders ($M = .79$, $SD = .32$) condoned exclusion more often than did 4th graders ($M = .90$, $SD = .23$) in the peer group context, $p < .012$. Closer analysis of between-subjects effects revealed that grade differences were specific to two scenarios: peer group–gender, $F(2, 275) = 5.75$, $p < .004$, and friendship–race, $F(2, 275) = 3.89$, $p < .022$. When evaluating an all-boys music club's decision to not allow a girl to join, 10th graders said it was okay more often than did 4th graders, $p < .006$. Tenth graders were also more likely than 7th graders to judge a White child's decision to not be friends with a Black child as okay, $p < .039$ (for means, see Table 6).

Summary

Results for judgments of exclusion regarding social consensus indicated that in the context of social pressure, exclusion was viewed as wrong. The school context elicited responses condemning exclusion from virtually all participants. Social pressure was more effective regarding decisions to exclude others in the friendship context than in either the school context or the peer group context. With the exception of the school context, which was not differentiated based on the target, exclusion based on race was rejected more often than was exclusion based on gender. Tenth graders were more willing to condone excluding a girl from an all-boys music club and to condone excluding a Black child from friendship than were the younger participants.

What Types of Reasons Do Children Use to Accept or Reject Social Consensus?

As shown in Table 5, three justification categories, fairness, group functioning, and personal choice, were used most often by children and adolescents to reason about exclusion of a girl or a Black child from friendship, peer group, and school contexts after hearing that peers and peer cohorts viewed exclusion differently from the protagonist.

Do Reasons Regarding Social Consensus Vary by the Context of Exclusion?

As shown in Table 3, results confirmed our expectation that justifications vary by context. Fairness reasoning was used to reject social consensus across all contexts, with the highest frequency of use in the school context, $p < .001$. Children and adolescents also used personal choice justification, however it was used primarily for the friendship context, $p < .001$, whereas group functioning justification was used only for the peer group context, $p < .001$. Thus, when reasoning about social consensus, fairness and personal choice justifications were primarily used for the friendship context, and fairness and group functioning justifications were used the most for the peer group context.

For example, children used personal choice reasoning to reject social consensus when asked to evaluate whether friends could influence the decision to not hang out with a girl: "Well, it should be up to Tom, not his friends. His friends shouldn't really be telling him what to do. He should be his own person and do what he wants to" (10th-grade European-American girl), and, "It is his choice. He shouldn't listen to his friends, he should do whatever he thinks is correct. His friends shouldn't be making his decisions and he should do whatever he wants to do" (10th-grade African-American boy).

When asked about excluding a girl from an all-boys music club, a 10th-grade European-American girl explained:

> It doesn't matter what other people say. It is still the same basis. You have to keep your view even if different people's opinions are told to you. Like if a new person comes and is the captain of the club and says that I am not going to let girls in then that is not going to work. It is still against different people and you have to keep it in some order. If there was a good reason that was different from being a girl, okay. But if there isn't then they should let her in.

In contrast, this 10th-grade European-American girl used group functioning to justify why it is okay for the music club to exclude the girl:

> Maybe they don't want to have a club that has girls in it. Sometimes like it was a group of guys and I was a girl and I went rock climbing with them, I might not be as good as all of them. It would be harder for me and they don't want me. *So it's okay for the boys to not let Jessica join?* Yeah, she can start her own club.

Do Reasons Regarding Social Consensus Vary by the Target of Exclusion?

Justifications also varied by the target. As shown in Table 4, fairness reasoning was used about the same for exclusion of the race target and for the gender target, whereas group functioning and personal choice reasoning were used more often for the gender target than for the race target. Thus, when asked to evaluate others' opinions of whether it is okay or not okay to exclude on the basis of gender, children and adolescents were more likely to use nonmoral reasons to justify exclusion of a girl than to justify exclusion of a Black child.

This 7th-grade African-American male based his judgment of why it is wrong to exclude a Black child from friendship on the issue of equality (fairness): "It's not okay because I just don't like that just because he's Black, he can't hang out with him? That's not right because they're just equal; they just have different colored skin, that's all."

A 10th-grade African-American male addressed the differences between the two targets in this evaluation of why it is not okay to exclude based on race but okay to exclude based on gender:

> I think that hmm. No, I don't think that they should, I don't think that Jerry's right on that one, because it's not like he's a girl or anything. I mean if he were a girl, then it would be different because I mean, they can't do stuff together, they probably wouldn't relate on very many things, but I mean this is two fellas and they should be getting along and they *can* relate on a lot of stuff. So I mean I don't think it's right that he shouldn't hang out with a boy cause he's Black.

Do Reasons Regarding Social Consensus for Gender and Race Targets Vary by the Context of Exclusion?

As expected, participants viewed exclusion of a Black child as wrong more often than they did exclusion of a girl even when considering others' opinions about whether it was okay or not okay to exclude. For both friendship and peer group contexts, fairness was used more to reason about the exclusion of a Black child than about the exclusion of a girl; however, there were no differences for the school context (for means, see Table 5).

When asked, "What if the majority of the town says that he shouldn't be able to go to school?" children used reasoning based on fairness::

> It doesn't matter because everyone has a right to an education and you shouldn't judge people by the color of their skin. (African-American 7th-grade male)

I think the townspeople should get a reality check, they should realize that . . . . I mean if everyone in the town feels that the girls shouldn't have to go to school, then I mean in that town, she probably wouldn't be allowed to go to school, but I don't think it would be right for them to say that she couldn't. *How come?* Everyone has the same brain, everyone has the same capacity for knowledge, they should all be able to learn and get jobs and do everything the same. There is no reason why guys should be above girls or girls should be above guys. There is not really anything that different—thinking, being as smart or being able to work out different things. (10th-grade European-American female)

In contrast, nonmoral justifications were used more for reasoning about the exclusion of a girl and were limited to certain contexts. Personal choice reasoning was limited to the friendship context and used more to reason about the exclusion of a girl than of a Black child, $p <$ .001. Likewise, group functioning was primarily used for the peer group context, with higher use for the exclusion of a girl than of a Black child, $p <$ .03.

For example, when explaining why it was okay for an all-boys music club to exclude a girl from joining, children referred to the way clubs function:

They set the rules. They can think about it and change it and like see what others are saying that it's the right thing to do, but they can sets the rules as they want. (10th-grade European-American male)

Because it's their club and they can do what they want with it . . . it's not nice, you know? I don't think it is like, oh yeah that is fine, but it is their club, they made it. So why can't they keep it the way they want it? (10th-grade European-American female)

Are There Gender, Grade, or Ethnicity Differences for Reasoning Regarding Social Consensus?

As predicted, children's and adolescents' reasoning varied depending on their gender, grade, and ethnicity. Analyses of fairness revealed an overall grade effect, $F(2, 276) = 6.68$, $p < .001$, indicating an increase in use of fairness with age. Tenth and 7th graders ($Ms = .59, .61, SDs = .21, .20$, respectively) were more likely than 4th graders ($M = .48, SD = .24$) to reject social pressure, and view exclusion as a fairness issue. Furthermore, analyses of individual scenarios resulted in significant grade effects for two particular scenarios, peer group–race and school–race. For peer group–race and school–race scenarios, 7th graders ($Ms = .61, .92, SDs = .47, .26$, peer group–race and school–race, respectively) and 10th graders (*Ms* = .62, .93, *SDs* = .47, .25, for peer group–race and school–race, respectively) were more likely to use fairness than were 4th graders (*Ms* = .41, .71, *SDs* = .48, .44, for peer group–race and school–race, respectively) when reasoning about exclusion with regard to social consensus considerations.

As an example, a 10th-grade Latin-American female shared her insights on why a Black child should not be excluded from school:

> We have a Constitution now, and it's forming us. We should be able to, we have to stand united, not look at people because of their race. *What do you mean? Can you explain that a little bit more?* Like, if you see a homeless person, and they're light skinned, and you're Black, and they ask you for a dollar, and they're really hungry, and you know they've been there for many days, you should at least give them something, even if it's like nickel or something. You don't know what that person's been through. People have been through many things over these years, and every single race, and it's time for us to stand united. We shouldn't just be like "oh, we don't like him because he's Black, or we don't like him because he's White." That's not right, we have to stand united. . . . We need to do something about that, and we need to stop faking, we need everybody to come together.

As predicted, when evaluating the peer group–gender scenario, older children used more group functioning justification than did younger children, $F(14, 1932) = 2.42$, $p < .02$. Tenth graders ($M = .49$, $SD = .48$) were more likely to view exclusion as a group functioning issue than were 4th graders ($M = .33$, $SD = .45$), $p < .05$. In addition, gender by grade findings were significant only for the friendship context. For the friendship–gender scenario, 7th-grade ($M = .68$, $SD = .47$) and 10th-grade ($M = .63$, $SD = .47$) boys were more likely than 4th-grade boys ($M = .38$, $SD = .45$), $p < .05$, to view exclusion as a personal choice issue when asked to consider the opinion of a group of friends about whether it was okay or not okay to exclude a girl from friendship. For the friendship–race scenario, 10th-grade girls ($M = .40$, $SD = .47$) were less likely than 10th-grade boys ($M = .59$, $SD = .48$), $p < .05$, to view exclusion of a Black boy from being friends with a White boy as a personal choice issue when social consensus was a factor to consider.

Summary

As predicted, when asked to consider others' opinions about whether it was okay or not okay to exclude a girl or Black child from friendship, peer group, and school contexts, children's and adolescents' reasoning varied depending on context, target, and participant variables. Overall, the use of fairness reasoning increased with age, with older children more likely to justify exclusion as unfair even when counterprobed with others' opinions about the legitimacy of exclusion. As expected, group functioning was used for the peer group context. More specifically, for the peer group–gender scenario older children were more likely to view exclusion in terms of group functioning. In contrast, personal choice reasons were used in the friendship context, with older boys being more likely to use personal choice to legitimize exclusion. This finding confirmed our hypothesis that boys, compared to girls, would more likely view the decision of a boy excluding a girl from friendship as up to the individual to decide.

How Does Authority Influence Children's Judgments of Exclusion?

Do Judgments Regarding Authority Influence Vary by the Context of Exclusion?

The second external influence assessment, authority influence, asked participants to evaluate the decision to exclude after considering an authority figure's recommendation or condemnation of exclusion. A context main effect, $F(2, 544) = 18.53$, $p < .001$, revealed that the school context ($M = .88$, $SD = .27$) was more often viewed as wrong to exclude in than was either the friendship context ($M = .73$, $SD = .34$) or the peer group context ($M = .80$, $SD = .30$), $ps < .001$.

Do Judgments Regarding Authority Influence Vary by the Target of Exclusion?

Analyses examining the effect of the target of exclusion, while controlling for the context, revealed a main effect for the target, $F(1, 272) = 61.79$, $p < .001$. Excluding a Black child ($M = .88$, $SD = .23$) was more likely to be evaluated as not okay than was excluding a girl ($M = .73$, $SD = .29$).

Do Judgments for Gender and Race Targets Regarding Authority Influence Vary by the Context of Exclusion?

A Context × Target interaction was found for the authority influence question, $F(2, 544) = 12.17$, $p < .001$. As shown in Table 7, excluding a Black child from school and excluding a girl from school were viewed as equally wrong; however, the two targets were differentiated in the friendship and peer group scenarios, with exclusion based on race judged as not okay more often than exclusion based on gender, $ps < .001$.

A Context × Target interaction revealed that excluding a girl from an all-boys music club was evaluated as not okay more often than was not

TABLE 7

PROPORTION OF NEGATIVE JUDGMENTS FOR AUTHORITY INFLUENCE

	Friendship Context				Peer Group Context				School Context			
	Gender		Race		Gender		Race		Gender		Race	
	M	SD	M	SD	M	SD	M	SD	M	SD	M	SD
Grade 4												
European-American	.58	(.50)	.92	(.27)	.76	(.44)	.96	(.20)	.85	(.37)	.85	(.37)
African-American	.58	(.50)	.73	(.45)	.67	(.48)	.79	(.42)	.79	(.42)	.88	(.33)
Other Minority	.71	(.46)	.83	(.38)	.80	(.41)	.88	(.33)	.68	(.48)	.76	(.44)
Total	.61	(.49)	.82	(.39)	.73	(.44)	.87	(.34)	.77	(.42)	.83	(.37)
Grade 7												
European-American	.63	(.49)	.88	(.33)	.83	(.38)	.90	(.30)	.93	(.26)	.93	(.26)
African-American	.62	(.50)	.86	(.36)	.81	(.40)	.86	(.36)	.80	(.41)	.71	(.46)
Other Minority	.64	(.49)	.82	(.39)	.68	(.48)	.95	(.21)	.86	(.35)	.91	(.29)
Total	.63	(.49)	.86	(.35)	.79	(.41)	.90	(.30)	.88	(.33)	.87	(.34)
Grade 10												
European-American	.64	(.48)	.79	(.42)	.67	(.48)	.88	(.33)	.95	(.22)	1.0	(.00)
African-American	.64	(.48)	.86	(.35)	.58	(.49)	.86	(.35)	.86	(.35)	.95	(.22)
Other Minority	.64	(.48)	.86	(.35)	.62	(.49)	.95	(.22)	.93	(.26)	.93	(.26)
Total	.64	(.48)	.83	(.37)	.62	(.48)	.90	(.31)	.91	(.28)	.96	(.20)
Total	.63	(.48)	.84	(.37)	.70	(.46)	.89	(.31)	.86	(.34)	.90	(.30)

Note.—N = 294. Proportions cannot exceed 1.00. Standard deviations are in parentheses.

being friends with a girl, $p < .048$. Likewise, the peer group and friendship contexts were differentiated when the target was a Black child. Not being friends with someone because he's Black was judged as okay more often than was not letting a Black child into an all-White music club, $p < .005$ (for all means, see Table 7).

Are There Gender, Grade, or Ethnicity Differences for Judgments Regarding Authority Influence?

Age-related findings for the authority question indicated that with age, participants rejected the authority in the school context, $F(4, 544) = 3.89$, $p < .004$. Tenth graders ($M = .94$, $SD = .21$) were more likely than 4th graders ($M = .80$, $SD = .33$) to reject the government's approval of excluding either a girl or a Black child from school, $p < .001$. This grade effect was contrary to the findings for the other assessments. Though 10th graders were more willing to exclude someone in the friendship–gender and peer group–gender scenarios and to be influenced by social consensus than were younger children, the younger participants were more

65

accepting of exclusion when condoned by the government than were 10th graders. Further analyses revealed that this was true of both the school–gender scenario and the school–race scenario, $ps < .028$ (for means, see Table 7). Grade differences were also found in the peer group–gender scenario, $F(2, 272) = 2.96$, $p < .054$. This difference followed the previous pattern, with 10th graders more likely than 7th graders to evaluate excluding a girl from an all-boys music club as okay, $p < .037$ (see Table 7).

An ethnicity effect for the peer group–race scenario, $F(2, 272) = 4.43$, $p < .013$, was also found. As shown in Table 7, when evaluating the decision of an all-White music club to not allow a Black child to join based solely on his race, African-American participants were more likely than Other Minority participants to judge this action as okay, $p < .019$.

Gender × Ethnicity × Grade interactions were significant for the school–gender scenario, $F(4, 272) = 2.66$, $p < .033$, and the school–race scenario, $F(4, 272) = 2.58$, $p < .038$. Tenth-grade African-American males ($M = 0.69$, $SD = 0.48$) were more likely then their European-American ($M = 0.89$, $SD = 0.32$) or Other Minority ($M = 0.89$, $SD = 0.32$) counterparts to judge excluding a girl from school as okay when approved by the government. Tenth-grade African-American females ($M = 0.96$, $SD = 0.20$), on the other hand, rejected authority influence and were more likely then 10th-grade African-American males ($M = 0.69$, $SD = 0.48$) to evaluate exclusion from school based on gender as wrong even when the government said it was allowed, $p < .013$. Follow-up analyses of the interaction in the school–race scenario revealed that the judgments of 7th-grade females differed by ethnicity, with African-American females ($M = 0.67$, $SD = 0.49$) more willing than European-American females ($M = 0.95$, $SD = 0.21$) or Other Minority females ($M = 1.00$, $SD = 0.00$) to judge the exclusion of a Black child from school as okay, $ps < .042$. There was also a significant difference between the judgments of 4th-grade European-American males ($M = 0.69$, $SD = 0.48$) and 4th-grade European-American females ($M = 1.00$, $SD = 0.00$), $p < .030$.

Summary

After considering the opinion of an authority figure on whether or not to exclude, participants viewed exclusion in the school context as more wrong than exclusion in the friendship or peer group contexts. Children and adolescents further stated that the friendship context was the more legitimate context for exclusion. Exclusion based on race was rejected more than exclusion based on gender, with the exception of the school context, in which exclusion was rejected as similar rates for both targets. Tenth graders were less convinced by governmental approval of exclusion from school than were 4th graders. However, 10th graders were more likely than 7th graders to agree with the all-boys music club's decision to not allow a girl to join. Ethnicity interacted with grade and gender revealing an increased acceptance by some African-Americans of exclusion in the school scenarios.

What Types of Reasons Do Children Give for Their Judgments About Authority Influence?

Five justification categories (fairness, empathy, group functioning, authority, and personal choice) were used most often by children and adolescents to reason about exclusion of a girl or a Black child from friendship, peer group, and school contexts after hearing counterprobes of authority figures' opinions about whether exclusion was okay or not okay (see Table 5).

Do Reasons Regarding Authority Influence Vary by the Context of Exclusion?

As predicted, children and adolescents used fairness when reasoning against authority influence across all contexts, however it was used the most for the school context, $p < .001$. In addition, empathy and personal choice reasoning were used primarily for the friendship context, ps $< .01$, group functioning reasoning was used only for the peer group context, $p < .001$, and authority justification was used about the same across the three contexts (see Table 3 for all means).

An example of authority is from a 4th-grade European-American boy who said, "Well, it's okay because you should listen to your parents. You should obey them. But he can just tell her that his parents said no so she won't feel bad about it."

In contrast, an African-American 4th grade girl gave priority to fairness: "The parents are teaching their son not to like people like that and like they are just doing wrong things and stuff just only to like White people and not Black people, and that's not right."

Yet, some children used both authority and fairness reasoning when asked to consider parents' influence on whether Damon should be friends with a girl. For example, a European-American 4th grader explained,

> I don't think it's right to do something that your parents don't want you to do, but still you should be friends with everyone. Maybe his parents had a good reason for telling him it was okay to not play with Damon (who is Black).

A European-American 7th-grade boy said: "You should probably listen to your parents. Cause they are normally right." Yet, another

European-American 7th-grade boy said: "No, just because someone else says that it's okay doesn't mean they have to agree or even that it is right. They should talk to her about it and decide something that is beneficial to both of them."

Do Reasons Regarding Authority Influence Vary by the Target of Exclusion?

Children's reasons varied by the target for the fairness, group functioning, and personal choice categories. There were no differences in the way children and adolescents used empathy and authority between targets. As shown in Table 4, despite authority influence considerations, fairness reasoning was used more for exclusion of the race target than of the gender target, $p < .001$, whereas group functioning and personal choice were used more often to reason about exclusion of the gender target than of the race target, $ps < .02$.

An Asian-American 10th grader explained why she believed excluding a Black child from an all-White music club would be wrong even if the parents encouraged it:

> I strongly don't like people that are so racist about things. I mean, it's so weird because like when I was growing up as a kid, my parents were always racist against different, I mean, they are not really racist, but they didn't like how I hung out with people form different countries and different cultures. I mean it's just not right to be racist, everyone is created equal and everyone is the same in the inside, it's just, we are unique in the outside. We are alike, there is just no reason for anyone should be eliminated from like anything just because of the way they look or their sex or the color of their skin.

Do Reasons Regarding Authority Influence for Gender and Race Targets Vary by the Context of Exclusion?

It was also hypothesized that children and adolescents would differ in their reasoning about excluding a girl or a Black boy between particular scenarios when asked to evaluate an authority figure's opinion of whether it was okay or not okay to exclude someone. As expected, for both friendship and peer group contexts, fairness was used more to reason about the exclusion of a Black child than for the exclusion of a girl, $ps < .001$ (see Table 5). However, for the school context, a vast majority of participants viewed exclusion as equally unfair for both scenarios, as illustrated in the following examples:

> They should just keep fighting until you get what you want and it might take a whole life time but at least you will get what you want, which is that all

children can go to school. The government is wrong to say that they can't go. (7th-grade European-American female)

We're all equal and we all deserve the same education, I mean, most of us deserve the same thing especially an education. (10th-grade African-American female)

I guess she has no choice but she should get a tutor or something, maybe home-schooled. But really, she should be allowed to get a public education. (10th-grade European-American male)

In contrast, nonmoral justifications were used more for reasoning about the exclusion of a girl and pertained specifically to certain contexts. Reasoning based on group functioning was primarily used for the peer group context, with higher use for exclusion of a girl than of a Black child, $p < .001$. Likewise, when personal choice was used, it was for the friendship context, and used more to reason about the exclusion of a girl than of a Black child, $p < .001$. Finally, authority was primarily used for both the friendship and peer group contexts with higher use for the exclusion of a girl than of a Black child, $ps < .001$ (for all means, see Table 5).

An example of the use of group functioning in the peer group context is the following from a European-American 10th-grade boy who stressed the autonomy of the club from the source of authority influence: "His parents aren't running the club. They are running the club and it's their decision. The boys should be the only ones to decide." A girl of the same age and ethnicity, however, focused on moral considerations: "Parents are not always right. It's not okay to be sexist and they're being very small-minded about it."

Are There Gender, Grade, or Ethnicity Differences for Reasoning Regarding Authority Influence?

As expected, significant findings were found for the use of justifications by the gender, grade, and ethnicity of the participants. When use of the fairness justification was examined, an overall grade effect was found, $F(2, 276) = 11.56$, $p < .001$, indicating that 7th ($M = .60$, $SD = .26$) and 10th ($M = .62$, $SD = .24$) graders were more likely to use fairness to reject authority influence than were 4th graders ($M = .44$, $SD = .25$), $p < .001$.

For example, when asked about parents' influence on an all-White boys' club excluding a Black child, a 7th-grade European-American girl replied:

It wouldn't matter what his parents said. If he lets him in, it's not going to be a punishment. Then he could just let him in because his parents don't know what this Black kid is like. So how can they judge him just because he's Black?

Fairness reasoning was also used to reject authority influence when it came to excluding a Black child from school. A 10th-grade Latin-American boy explained:

It's not okay, but the government's the government. *What do you mean?* Because they're actually the power in this, in the U.S. They're the ones who give the funds for the schools and everything. *Do you think it's okay for them to do that?* No. *Why?* Because they're letting a person not to learn just because their race. It shouldn't be like that. *Why?* It's gonna be like a racist government. What's the point of having that? People come here from other countries, like ancestors, just to have a better life. But so you can come here and stop doing all that stupid crap again a lot, back in the time where you can't go just cause you're Black and all that other stuff, it ain't right.

A closer examination of individual scenarios indicated that this age trend was significant for the school–gender, friendship–race, peer group–race, and school–race scenarios, $ps < .05$ (for means, see Table 5). In addition, for the friendship–race scenario, an ethnicity effect, $F(14, 1932) = 2.79$, $p < .001$, was also significant. African-Americans ($M = 0.45$, $SD = 0.48$) used fairness reasoning less frequently than did European-Americans ($M = 0.62$, $SD = 0.46$), $p < .04$. Upon closer examination of why African-American children's use of fairness was significantly less, it was revealed that reasoning based on empathy was used more often by African-American children ($M = 0.06$, $SD = 0.20$) than by European-American children ($M = 0.02$, $SD = 0.13$), $p < .05$.

When we examined the use of empathy, we found an overall between-subjects grade effect, $F(2, 276) = 16.52$, $p < .001$, indicating that across all scenarios, empathy use decreased with age. Compared to the 7th ($M = .02$, $SD = .05$) and 10th graders ($M = .01$, $SD = 0.03$), $p < .001$, the 4th graders ($M = .08$, $SD = .14$) used more empathy to reason against an authority's mandate of exclusion. Closer analyses of scenarios indicated that this age pattern was significant for the friendship–race scenario ($M = .13$, $SD = .31$, for 4th grade; $M = .04$, $SD = .17$, for 7th grade; $M = .02$, $SD = .11$, for 10th grade), the peer group–race scenario ($M = .11$, $SD = .31$, for 4th grade; $M = .01$, $SD = .11$, for 7th grade; $M = .00$, $SD = .00$, for 10th grade), and the school–race scenario ($M = .05$, $SD = .21$, for 4th grade; $M = .00$, $SD = .00$, for 7th grade; $M = .00$, $SD = .04$, for 10th grade), $ps < .05$.

Also, as predicted, an overall between-subjects grade effect was found in the use of authority reasoning, $F(2, 276) = 7.59$, $p < .01$, as was an overall ethnicity effect, $F(2, 276) = 5.61$, $p < .01$. Use of authority justification decreased with age, with 4th graders ($M = .20$, $SD = .23$) referring more to authority mandates to justify exclusion than did 10th graders ($M = .09$, $SD = .19$), $p < .05$. Follow-up analyses on individual scenarios indicated that this age pattern was significant for both the friendship–race ($M = .14$, $SD = .34$, for 4th grade; $M = .03$, $SD = .16$, for 10th grade) and the peer group–race ($M = .13$, $SD = .34$, for 4th grade; $M = .03$, $SD = .16$, for 10th grade) scenarios, $ps < .05$. Regarding ethnicity effects, Other Minority children ($M = .18$, $SD = .24$) used authority to justify exclusion more than did European-American children ($M = .09$, $SD = .14$), $p < .05$. Follow-up analyses revealed this pattern to be significant for the peer group–gender scenario, with Other Minority children ($M = .21$, $SD = .42$) validating authority justification more than did European-American children ($M = .08$, $SD = .27$), $p < .05$, when reasoning about the exclusion of a girl from an all-boys music club.

Finally, for use of the personal choice justification, an ethnicity effect, $F(14, 1932) = 3.29$, $p < .001$, was found for the friendship–gender scenario. European-Americans children ($M = .60$, $SD = .48$) rejected the authority's influence on the decision to exclude by using personal choice reasoning (it is up to the individual to decide) more than did African-American children ($M = .37$, $SD = .48$) and Other Minority children ($M = .42$, $SD = .49$), $p < .05$.

Summary

Children's and adolescents' reasoning about the influence of authority on the exclusion of an individual varied as a function of the context, target, and participant variables. Overall, fairness reasoning was used by a majority of individuals to reject authority influence on the exclusion of a Black child across all contexts and for the exclusion of a girl from school. Older children were more likely to use fairness to reason about exclusion than were younger children. Although not used frequently, empathy was more likely to be used by younger children to reason about exclusion than by older children, and African-American children were more likely to use empathy to reject authority influence as a legitimate reason for exclusion. In addition, European-American children viewed exclusion from friendship as a personal choice decision more often than did children from other ethnicities. Finally, authority reasoning was used to justify exclusion across all three contexts equally and more often for the exclusion of a girl than of a Black child. With age, younger children were more influenced by an authority figure's opinion on whether exclusion was okay or not okay.

Do Children Generalize Their Judgments of Exclusion to Other Countries?

Do Judgments Regarding Generalizability Vary by the Context of Exclusion?

The third external influence assessment asked children and adolescents to evaluate the acts of exclusion if they were to occur in another country. Analyses of the generalizability assessment revealed a main effect for context, $F(2, 536) = 36.71$, $p < .001$. Participants were more likely to evaluate the exclusion of an individual from school ($M = 0.91$, $SD = 0.23$) in another country as wrong than to evaluate exclusion from friendship ($M = 0.70$, $SD = 0.36$) or peer group ($M = 0.76$, $SD = 0.34$) in another country as wrong, $ps < .001$.

Do Judgments Regarding Generalizability Vary by the Target of Exclusion?

Across contexts, children and adolescents were more likely to generalize the wrongfulness of excluding a Black child ($M = .87$, $SD = .25$) than the wrongfulness of excluding a girl ($M = .71$, $SD = .30$), $F(1, 268) = 81.04$, $p < .001$. In other words, more children judged excluding a Black child in another country as wrong than judged excluding a girl in another country as wrong.

Do Judgments for Gender and Race Targets Regarding Generalizability Vary by the Context of Exclusion?

A Context × Target interaction, $F(1, 273) = 55.04$, $p < .001$, qualified the main effect for context. Closer analysis of the scenarios revealed that for the gender target, and consistent with the main effect for context, the school context was viewed as the least legitimate condition for exclusion, $p < .001$. Further distinction, however, was made between the friendship–gender and the peer group–gender scenarios, with excluding a girl from friendship judged as okay more often than excluding a girl from a music club, $p < .019$. The scenarios involving exclusion based on race were consistent with the main effect for context; exclusions in the friendship and peer group scenarios were not differentiated but were more likely to be evaluated as okay than exclusion in the school scenario, $p < .001$ (see Table 8 for all means).

Analyses of the scenarios also revealed that, unlike the findings for the previous questions, the school context was differentiated by the target of exclusion in terms of generalizability. As shown in Table 8, the vast

TABLE 8

PROPORTION OF NEGATIVE JUDGMENTS FOR GENERALIZABILITY

	Friendship Context				Peer Group Context				School Context			
	Gender		Race		Gender		Race		Gender		Race	
	M	SD	M	SD	M	SD	M	SD	M	SD	M	SD
Grade 4												
Female	.56	(.50)	.77	(.42)	.77	(.42)	.85	(.36)	.94	(.24)	.87	(.34)
Male	.66	(.48)	.83	(.38)	.60	(.50)	.89	(.32)	.86	(.35)	.94	(.23)
Total	.60	(.49)	.80	(.40)	.70	(.46)	.87	(.34)	.90	(.30)	.90	(.30)
Grade 7												
Female	.60	(.49)	.93	(.26)	.83	(.38)	.84	(.37)	.81	(.39)	.95	(.21)
Male	.63	(.49)	.88	(.33)	.66	(.48)	.90	(.30)	.93	(.27)	1.0	(.00)
Total	.62	(.49)	.90	(.30)	.75	(.44)	.87	(.34)	.87	(.34)	.98	(.15)
Grade 10												
Female	.62	(.49)	.79	(.41)	.60	(.49)	.86	(.35)	.89	(.31)	.92	(.28)
Male	.45	(.50)	.75	(.43)	.57	(.50)	.75	(.43)	.83	(.38)	.96	(.19)
Total	.55	(.50)	.78	(.42)	.59	(.49)	.82	(.39)	.86	(.34)	.94	(.24)
Total	.58	(.49)	.82	(.39)	.66	(.47)	.85	(.36)	.88	(.33)	.94	(.24)

Note.—$N = 294$. Proportions cannot exceed 1.00. Standard deviations are in parentheses.

majority of children and adolescents generalized the wrongfulness of excluding a Black child from school in another country. Fewer participants, on the other hand, evaluated the exclusion of a girl from school in another country as wrong, $p < .001$.

Are There Gender, Grade, or Ethnicity Differences for Judgments About Generalizability?

Tests of overall between-subjects effects revealed a grade effect, $F(2, 268) = 3.47$, $p < .033$. Tenth graders ($M = .75$, $SD = .25$) were less likely than 7th graders ($M = .84$, $SD = .19$) to generalize the wrongfulness of exclusion to other countries, $p < .032$. Univariate analyses indicated that grade differences in the peer group–gender and friendship–race scenarios were driving this effect. When evaluating the decision of an all-boys music club in another country to not allow a girl to join, 10th graders were more likely than 7th graders to judge this decision as okay, $p < .044$. Likewise, 10th graders were more condoning than 7th graders of the decision of someone in another country to not be friends with someone because he's Black, $p < .051$ (for means, see Table 8).

A gender effect, $F(1, 268) = 7.04$, $p < .008$, was also found for the peer group–gender scenario. Females ($M = .71$, $SD = .45$) were more likely

73

than were males ($M = .60$, $SD = .50$) to evaluate the exclusion of a girl from an all-boys music club in another country as wrong, $p < .008$. This effect was further qualified by a Gender × Ethnicity interaction in the peer group–gender scenario, $F(2, 268) = 3.17$, $p < .043$. For the Other Minority sample, females ($M = .76$, $SD = .43$) were more likely than were males ($M = .50$, $SD = .51$) to generalize the wrongfulness of exclusion, $p < .012$.

Summary

When evaluating the act of exclusion in another country, children and adolescents were more likely to generalize the wrongfulness of exclusion when the target was a Black child than when the target was a girl. Exclusion from school was considered wrong more often than exclusion from friendship and from a music club. Younger participants were more likely than older participants to evaluate exclusion in another country negatively. Females and males differed with respect to whether it was okay or not for an all-boys music club in another country to not allow a girl to join, with females rejecting the decision to exclude more often than males.

What Types of Reasons Do Children Give for Their Judgments About Exclusion in Another Country?

As shown in Table 5, five justification categories (fairness, empathy, group functioning, social tradition, and personal choice) were used most often by children and adolescents to reason about exclusion of a girl or a Black child from friendship, peer group, and school contexts after they were asked to consider whether exclusion would be okay or not okay in another country.

Do Reasons Regarding Generalizability Vary by the Context of Exclusion?

Results confirmed our expectations that children's and adolescents' use of justifications would vary by context when they evaluated exclusion in another country. As shown in Table 3, fairness reasoning was used by a majority of participants across all contexts; however, it was used the most for the school context, $p < .001$. In addition, empathy and personal choice justifications were used primarily for the friendship context, $ps < .01$, group functioning was used only for the peer group context, $p < .001$, and social tradition was used more for the friendship and peer group contexts than for the school context, $p < .01$.

For example, some children appealed to another country's social traditions to justify why it was okay to exclude either a girl or a Black child:

> It will depend on the country because there are some countries where girls and boys are completely different. Like boys go play the same game and girls sew whatever, and then in another country if they were doing the same thing, it would be okay. (7th-grade European-American female)

> In another country . . . I don't know, they are different, they could have different cultures in another country, like in Japan, schools are practically 90% Japanese and then here you know it's like what 30% White, so in Japan there is a lot less diversity and they probably are already racist to someone who goes to their school because they are the main majority. *So in other countries where there are different cultures and different rules, would it be okay or not okay for them to exclude?* It would probably be okay because they just, because it is up to them and they are taught different than we are, cause in the United States there is big diversity, but like any other country, it's not nearly as big. (10th-grade European-American male; peer group–race scenario)

In contrast, here are examples from participants of why it would be wrong to exclude a Black child from an all-White music club in another country:

> Everybody deserves the right of a chance to be in a club. Black people have gone through a lot and to have people just be treating them down even more is really hard for them, so everybody should just really try to get to know people no matter what their race is because, well, it makes us really unique. (European-American 4th-grade female)

> Because that is bad, too. We want world peace here, so everyone should be friends with everybody. . . . that way we don't have to spend money on bombs and stuff and we could spend money on food and clothes. *So even if the rules are different there and that's just the way people think—just like we want everyone to be equal and we think that's right—What if there they think Black people are not equal, then would that be okay?* No, because here they used to think Black people weren't equal, but then now they are getting around to knowing that we are, so that's how other countries should be going. (10th-grade African-American female)

Do Reasons Regarding Generalizability Vary by the Target of Exclusion?

Justifications also varied by the target of exclusion. As shown in Table 4, when participants were asked to evaluate exclusion in another country, they more often used fairness as justification for the race target than for the gender target, $p < .001$. In contrast, group functioning, social tradition, and personal choice categories were used more often to reason about

75

exclusion in another country for the gender target than for the race target, $ps < .001$.

As an example, a 10th-grade Indian-American male used social tradition and group functioning to explain why excluding a girl from a music club would be okay in another country:

> I guess the same rules apply, but in other countries, like, they would have girls, I think they would have separate clubs. Like in India, boys and girls don't interact. *Okay so that's a good example, so do you think it is okay if they do that, if boys and girls don't interact, is it okay that the boys have a club that is all boys?* Yeah. *How come you think that it's okay?* Because I think they don't know how to interact because they never do so. It would be really weird if there was a girl in there. *So what would be the consequences if someone made them have a club that was boys and girls?* I don't know, they might just like not include her in anything, just like talk amongst themselves and she would be like all alone and feel really weird. *So do you think it would be even worse if they made her join the club?* Yeah, probably.

Do Reasons Regarding Generalizability for Gender and Race Targets Vary by the Context of Exclusion?

As hypothesized, children and adolescents differed in their reasoning about excluding a girl or a Black boy between particular scenarios when asked to evaluate whether it was okay or not okay to exclude in another country. Results were only significant for use of the fairness, group functioning, and personal choice reasons. Participants did not differ in their use of empathy and social tradition. As expected, for both friendship and peer group contexts, fairness was used more to reason about the exclusion of a Black child than about the exclusion of a girl, $ps < .001$ (for means, see Table 5). However, for the school context, a vast majority of participants viewed exclusion as equally unfair for both scenarios.

As an example, a 10th-grade Latin-American boy shares his view on why it is unfair for a Black child to be excluded from an all-White music club in another country:

> I think they, no matter what they think, should let him join. But sometimes you can't do anything about it, but in my opinion, I would let him in, if I were in that case. *Okay and why would you let him join?* Because you think there's nothing wrong with another country, because like, for example, I'm not, I wasn't born here, I'm from Guatemala, and like if when I came to school the Americans in the school, nobody said anything 'cause I'm Spanish, then I think I would feel bad, the same would be if someone from here had

to move down to Central America or some other country and they were treated just because they were different, from a different country.

This 10th-grade Latin-American boy first reasoned that exclusion based on race is okay but then changed his mind:

How could it be okay? Because maybe they were brought up like that or raised like that and do that. Like let's say White kids did something or White people did something to make themselves look bad. So you know they raised their kids saying don't hang around White kids. *Do you think that's okay? Do you think it's a good reason not to like a group of people because that's they way you were brought up?* No, because we should all see each other as one. Because we're . . . count on each other to help each other. Like when I need help, I can go maybe to my friend, he's Black, he won't know I need to know, what if my friend who's White knows . . . so you can't always be around the same people because they won't like have the same points of view and if you, you think like them, then it will be kind of crazy, but if you have somebody else who can suggest something or who can, you can learn from, that's better.

In contrast, nonmoral justifications were used more for reasoning about the exclusion of a girl and were limited to certain contexts. Group functioning justification was primarily used for the peer group context, and more frequently for exclusion of a girl than exclusion of a Black child, $p < .001$. Likewise, personal choice, was limited to one context, friendship, and used more to reason about the exclusion of a girl than of a Black child, $p < .001$ (for means, see Table 5).

Are There Gender, Grade, or Ethnicity Differences for Reasoning Regarding Generalizability?

It was hypothesized that children's and adolescents' reasoning about exclusion in another country would vary depending on their gender, grade, or ethnicity. Results confirmed our expectations. An overall grade effect was significant in the use of fairness as justification for exclusion, $F(2, 276) = 5.08$, $p < .01$, with 7th ($M = .72$, $SD = .22$) and 10th ($M = .67$, $SD = .26$) graders applying fairness to another country more frequently than did 4th graders ($M = .58$, $SD = .21$), $p < .05$. A closer examination of individual scenarios indicated that this age trend was significant for the friendship–race scenario ($M = .51$, $SD = .48$, for 4th grade; $M = .76$, $SD = .43$, for 7th grade; $M = .69$, $SD = .46$, for 10th grade), $p < .01$. In addition, ethnicity effects were found for the friendship–race, $F(14, 1932) = 2.91$, $p < .001$, and school–gender, $F(14, 1932) = 2.32$, $p < .01$, scenarios. For both of these scenarios, European-American children ($Ms = .75$, .88,

SDs = .42, .31, respectively, for friendship–race and school–gender) applied fairness to other countries slightly more than did African-American children (Ms = .56, .76, SDs = .49, .43, respectively, for friendship–race and school–gender).

The use of empathy in reasoning about exclusion also showed an overall between-subjects grade effect, $F(2, 276) = 16.47$, $p < .001$. Although used infrequently across all scenarios, references to empathy decreased with age. Compared to 7th ($M = .02$, $SD = .06$) and 10th graders ($M = .01$, $SD = .03$), $p < .001$, 4th graders ($M = .07$) used empathy more often to justify why an individual should not be excluded in another country. Closer analyses of scenarios indicated that this age pattern was significant for the peer group–gender scenario ($M = .08$, $SD = .25$, for 4th grade; $M = .02$, $SD = .09$, for 7th grade; $M = .02$, $SD = .13$, for 10th grade) and the peer group–race scenario ($M = .10$, $SD = .29$, for 4th grade; $M = .01$, $SD = .11$, for 7th grade; $M = .00$, $SD = .00$, for 10th grade), $ps < .05$.

Similarly, the use of group functioning in reasoning about exclusion showed overall between-subjects grade, $F(2, 276) = 3.86$, $p < .02$, and gender effects, $F(1, 276) = 4.58$, $p < .03$. The use of group functioning to reason about exclusion in another country increased with age. Tenth graders ($M = .06$, $SD = .09$) viewed exclusion in another country as a group functioning issue more than did 7th graders ($M = .03$, $SD = .06$), $p < .05$. In addition, boys ($M = .06$, $SD = .09$) used group functioning slightly more than did girls ($M = .04$, $SD = .08$), $p < .05$.

When children's and adolescents' use of social tradition to justify exclusion in another country was examined, the only significant finding was for the rights–gender context, indicated by a grade-by-gender effect, $F(14, 1932) = 2.00$, $p < .02$. Seventh-grade girls ($M = .19$, $SD = .39$) used social tradition to justify exclusion more than did 4th-grade girls ($M = .02$, $SD = .14$), $p < .05$. In addition, 4th-grade boys ($M = .14$, $SD = .35$) justified exclusion using social tradition more than did 4th-grade girls ($M = .02$, $SD = .14$), $p < .05$. Finally, an overall gender effect was significant for the use of personal choice, $F(2, 276) = 3.00$, $p < .05$, indicating that boys ($M = .08$, $SD = .11$) were more likely to use personal choice to justify exclusion in another country than were girls ($M = .06$, $SD = .10$), $p < .05$.

Although, as stated above, social tradition was used to justify excluding girls from school in another country, some participants who came from other countries denied social tradition as a legitimate reason for not allowing girls to get an education and, instead, used fairness, as illustrated in the following examples:

> I still don't agree with that, like where I am from, I am from Vietnam, people still think girls shouldn't be educated. I think girls should be educated, like, we have every right to be educated. I think education is really, really impor-

tant because we need that for everything. I mean, just to read and write. I think that's just really, really important. I can't imagine myself not being able to read and write because that's just one of the ways to communicate and I think no matter where you are from or where you are living at, I think education is still really, really important. (10th-grade Asian-American female)

In my country, the girls don't have to go to school. They don't have to go to school. Probably more go than, but, in my family every single girl went. Most of them wanted to. *What if a country says the girls can't go to school, do you think that's okay for them to say that?* In another country for them not to go to school? No, that wouldn't be okay because I mean all the guys can learn everything, and [the girls] can't. It's like the guys are hogging everything. So, I don't know, in another country, I think that wouldn't be good. (10th-grade Latin-American female)

Summary

As hypothesized, children's and adolescents' reasoning about the exclusion of an individual in another country varied depending on context, target, and participant variables. Overall, when the fairness justification was applied to decisions regarding another country, it was used across all contexts and targets, and its frequency of use increased with age, as older children were more likely to view exclusion in terms of fairness than were younger children. Empathy was used, although infrequently, more often by younger children and African-American children to reject exclusion in another country. In addition, when social tradition reasoning was used, it was by older girls to justify the exclusion of girls in another country from attending school. Group functioning was used in the peer group context more often by older children and by boys who said it was okay to exclude to preserve social coordination. Finally, personal choice was predominately used in the friendship context, with boys, when asked to generalize to another country, using personal choice reasons to justify exclusion slightly more than did girls.

CHANGE ASSESSMENT

Do Children Change Their Judgment About Exclusion as a Function of External Influences?

We conducted analyses to determine the extent to which social consensus, authority mandates, and cultural norms prompted children to change their judgments about exclusion. In other words, if children stated that it was wrong to exclude someone did they change their judgment upon hearing that a parent said it was all right to exclude someone? (or if their peers said it was all right to exclude someone? or if it occurred in another country?). We predicted that children would be influenced by social consensus more than by authority and cultural norms due to the fact that group functioning has been shown to be a strong concern of children and adolescents when evaluating exclusion (Killen & Stangor, 2001). Further, we made predictions about the direction of change. Based on prior findings (Killen et al., 2001) we expected that children who initially rejected exclusion would be more stable in their convictions than would children who initially condoned exclusion.

To conduct our statistical tests, we computed separate $2 \times 3 \times 3$ (Gender × Grade × Ethnicity) ANOVAs for each target (gender, race) and context (friendship, peer group, and school) on the proportion of students who changed their exclusion judgments in response to each of the external influence probes (see Chapter III, Method, for a description of how we created the change variables). Overall, most children stayed with their initial judgment and did not change their decision about exclusion after hearing the various external influence supporting or opposing point of view (82%; range from 74% to 97% across contexts).

As predicted, and as shown in Table 9, we found that in those instances when there was a change in judgment, the direction of change was more often toward the positive (rejecting exclusion) than toward the negative (condoning exclusion).

Social Consensus

As shown in Table 9, for social consensus, children became more inclusive rather than less inclusive when they were asked to consider the influence from friends, peers, and other townspeople. For the friendship and peer group contexts for the gender target, $Fs(1, 258) = 26.78$, 68.00, $ps < .0001$, and for the school context, $F(1, 272) = 76.38$, $p < .0001$, participants who changed their judgment did so in the positive direction (toward rejecting exclusion) more often than in the negative direction (toward accepting exclusion). The same findings were shown for the race target (for friendship, $F(1, 259) = 59.07$, $p < .001$, for peer group, $F(1, 260) = 77.07$, $p < .0001$, and for the school context, $F(1, 272) = 42.76$, $p < .0001$); participants changed more often to the positive direction than to the negative direction.

Follow-up tests revealed gender, grade, and ethnicity effects for these findings. For the peer group–gender scenario, more females ($M = .59$, $SD = .50$) who changed did so in a positive direction than did males ($M = .31$, $SD = .46$), $F(1, 258) = 13.27$, $p < .0001$, and the Other Minority group

TABLE 9

PROPORTION OF CHILDREN WHO CHANGED THEIR EXCLUSION JUDGMENT AFTER HEARING
THREE PROBES FOR THE GENDER AND RACE TARGETS BY CONTEXT

Probe and Direction of Change	Gender Target by Context			Race Target by Context		
	Friend M	Peer M	School M	Friend M	Peer M	School M
Social consensus						
From OK	.24**	.41**	.80**	.20**	.36**	.50**
to Not OK	(22 of 90)	(36 of 88)	(4 of 5)	(8 of 40)	(12 of 33)	(2 of 4)
From Not OK	.07	.04	.04	.08	.02	.02
to OK	(14 of 204)	(9 of 206)	(11 of 289)	(21 of 254)	(6 of 260)	(6 of 290)
Authority influence						
From OK	.29	.35**	.20	.35**	.45**	.50*
to Not OK	(26 of 90)	(31 of 88)	(1 of 5)	(14 of 40)	(15 of 33)	(2 of 4)
From Not OK	.22	.15	.12	.08	.05	.10
to OK	(44 of 204)	(30 of 206)	(36 of 289)	(21 of 254)	(14 of 261)	(28 of 290)
Generalizability						
From OK	.14	.26*	.00	.23**	.27**	.25**
to Not OK	(13 of 90)	(23 of 88)	(0 of 5)	(9 of 40)	(9 of 33)	(1 of 4)
From Not OK	.22	.17	.11	.09	.08	.05
to OK	(46 of 204)	(34 of 206)	(32 of 289)	(22 of 254)	(21 of 260)	(15 of 290)

Note.—*p < .01; **p < .001. Significance refers to the direction of change. N = 294. Friend = friendship context, Peer = peer group context, School = school context. Actual number of children who changed their judgment is listed in parentheses.

(M = .55, SD = .49) changed more than did the other two ethnic groups (Ms = .34, SD = .48 and .30, SD = .47 for European-American and African-American), $F(2, 258)$ = 6.83, p < .001. Because so few participants (5) had originally said it was OK to exclude in the school–gender scenario, even though 4 of them changed we do not report the participant findings for this context. For the friendship–race scenario, there was an ethnicity effect, $F(2, 259)$ = 20.02, p < .0001, with Asian-American and Latin-American participants (M = .38, SD = .50) changing in a positive direction more often than European-American (M = .00) or African-American participants (M = .25, SD = .45). The grade effect also revealed that 7th graders (M = .57, SD = .53) were more likely to change than were 4th (M = .22, SD = 0) or 10th graders (M = .08, SD = .28), $F(2, 259)$ = 15.23, p < .0001. Similarly, for the peer group–race scenario, African-American students (M = .43, SD = .51) were more likely to change than were European-American students (M = .27, SD = .46), $F(2, 260)$ = 9.70, p < .0001.

In summary, the findings for the social consensus source of influence revealed that if contemplating peer reactions to the exclusion resulted in a change in judgment it was more often a positive change regarding

81

children's judgments about exclusion. While most children did change, those children who said that it was all right to exclude someone were highly likely to change their judgment upon hearing that friends and peer cohorts encouraged the protagonist to be friends with the target, or include the target in the group. However, the reverse was not true. Children who rejected exclusion were highly unlikely to change their judgment and reject exclusion after hearing that friends and peer cohorts encouraged the protagonist to reject the target. Further, females and minority students were more likely to change their judgments in the positive direction after hearing probes than were males or European-American students; 7th graders were also significantly influenced by the probes.

Authority Influence

Children were less likely to be influenced by parents and the government (authority) than by friends and peers (social consensus). For the gender target, there were no significant differences between the two types of change; 29% changed from okay to not okay after hearing the authority probe, and 22% changed from not okay to okay after hearing the authority probe. Thus, participants were as likely to change in either direction when considering what a parent had to say about not being friends with someone based on gender. The same was true for the school context; considering what townspeople had to say about excluding girls from school did not influence participants in the positive direction more than in the negative direction. This was in contrast to the peer group context, however, in which more children changed to accept the girl in the music club after hearing that parents wanted the club to be inclusive than changed to reject the girl based on parental pressure, $F(1, 258) = 14.26$, $p < .0001$.

Yet, for the race target, authority had a positive influence on children's judgments for all three contexts, $Fs(1, 259; 1, 260; 1, 272) = 36.70$, 74.55, and 6.74, $ps < .0001$, $.001$, and $.01$, for friendship, peer group, and school. For the friendship context, there was an ethnicity effect, $F(2, 259) = 5.03$, $p < .007$; the authority probe influenced minority students ($Ms = .33$, $SD = .49$ and $.54$, $SD = .51$ for African-American and Other Minority) to change in the positive direction more than did European-American students ($M = .13$, $SD = .35$). Yet, for excluding a Black child from a music club, Other Minority students ($M = .67$, $SD = .57$) changed more positively than did African-Americans ($M = .25$, $SD = .46$) or European-American students ($M = .40$, $SD = .54$), $F(2, 260) = 8.5$, $p < .0001$.

In summary, few children and adolescents changed their judgments as a function of the authority probe, but, as predicted, authority was more influential for the minority than for the nonminority students, and particularly so for the race target scenarios.

Generalizability

Asking children whether exclusion was all right in another cultural context proved to be similar to the authority probe. Cultural norms did not change children's judgments in one direction more than in another direction for the friendship–gender and school–gender scenarios. This probe did, however, prompt children to change in the positive direction more than in the negative direction for the peer group context, $F(1, 258) = 8.98$, $p < .003$, and for all three race target scenarios ($Fs(1, 259; 1, 260; 1, 272) = 15.58, 8.60, 7.50$, $ps < .007$). As with the findings for the other sources of external influence, females were more likely to change in the positive direction than were males for the peer group–gender context: females: $M = .36$, $SD = .48$; males: $M = .16$, $SD = .16$, $F(1, 258) = 8.65$, $ps < .004$. Minority students were more likely to change in the positive direction than were nonminority students for the friendship–race scenario: European-American, $M = .00$; African-American: $M = .42$, $SD = .51$; Other Minority, $M = .31$, $SD = .48$, $F = (2, 259) = 7.28$, $p < .001$.

In summary, in contrast to what might be expected, that peers would be negatively influential and parents would be positively influential, social consensus from friends and peers was the most powerful form of external influence for prompting children and adolescents to change their judgments in the positive direction. Further, females were more likely to change in the positive direction in the gender target scenarios, and minorities were more likely to change in the positive direction for the race target scenarios. This indicated that identifying with the target of exclusion made one open to positive forms of external social influence.

V. DISCUSSION

> The dilemma of difference grows from the ways in which this
> society assigns individuals to categories and, on that basis, de-
> termines whom to include in and whom to exclude from po-
> litical, social, and economic activities.
>
> Martha Minow, *Making All the Difference:*
> *Inclusion, Exclusion, and American Law*

The changing demographics in the United States toward ethnic and
racial diversity have led developmental psychologists to give attention to
this phenomenon in both their research theories and agendas (Fisher
et al., 1998; National Research Council and Institute of Medicine, 2000).
One way to do this is to investigate children's awareness of gender, ethnicity, and racial diversity as reflected by their social attitudes, social cognition, and moral judgments. Another way to do this is to include children
from diverse backgrounds as participants in research studies. In this project,
we followed both courses of action. We examined how different forms of
knowledge—moral, social-conventional (stereotypes), and personal—are
brought to bear on children's decisions about exclusion based on gender
and race. In addition, we included as participants boys and girls from
four different ethnic backgrounds (Euro-American, African-American, Latin-
American, and Asian-American).

The findings discussed in this *Monograph* reveal quite clearly that children use multiple forms of reasoning when making decisions about exclusion, which confirms our theoretical proposal that exclusion is a
multifaceted phenomenon (Killen et al., 2002; Killen & Stangor, 2001).
Guided by a social-cognitive domain model, we found that children's evaluations of exclusion depend on the context and the target of exclusion,
as well as on the gender, age, and ethnicity of the individual making the
judgment. Social-cognitive domain theory indicates that social judgments
are sensitive to the context of social interactions, and that an analysis of
the context is necessary in order to determine patterns of social reasoning (see Helwig, 1995; Smetana, 1995; Turiel, 1983, 2002; Turiel et al.,
1987). We found that exclusion is not always viewed as a moral transgression, nor is it solely a matter of group functioning and conventions. There
are times when exclusion is considered wrong because it is unfair to in-

dividuals and denies them equal access to social relationships, groups, and institutions. At other times, exclusion is viewed as legitimate because it is a matter of individual choice (particularly in friendship contexts) or because it is necessary to make groups work well.

In fact, children at all the ages we included in this study made clear distinctions between exclusion in our three contexts, friendship, peer groups, and societal institutions such as school, and they used different forms of reasoning to evaluate exclusion in these contexts. As predicted, friendship is viewed as the most legitimate context in which someone could decide not to be friends with a peer solely on the basis of gender or race, and this is because friendship is viewed as a personal decision. We did not interview children about what criterion they used to make a friend, or how they evaluated the "goodness or badness" of using group membership, such as gender or race, as a criteria for picking a friend. This would be fruitful to examine in a follow-up study.

Based on what many children articulated spontaneously in their interviews, we predicted that the majority of participants would judge that using gender or race to make a decision about friendship is not a very good reason even in cases in which they viewed friendship as a personal decision. Many of the reasons they gave, however, may, in fact, be implicit forms of bias (not realized by the children). Given the extensive documentation of implicit and unconscious biases (racial and gender) found in adult studies (Gaertner & Dovidio, 1986), it is worthwhile to further examine children's and adolescents' statements about exclusion for evidence of biases. For example, children who stated that it was all right not to be friends with someone of a different race did so by stating that it was "up to the child to decide" (individual prerogative, coded as personal choice) and that they "probably didn't have the same interests" (individual preferences, coded as personal choice).

Yet, when Aboud et al. (in press) investigated children's cross-race friendships, they found that although cross-race friendships were fairly infrequent, the qualities attributed to those relationships were not significantly different from the qualities associated with same-race friendships. Thus, children's views that children from different races "may not share the same interests" may derive from their stereotypic thinking and not from actual experience. Children may be unaware that they hold unsubstantiated assumptions about the nature of cross-race friendships. Only a minority of participants used gender or race as the sole basis for excluding someone as a potential friend, but this type of judgment increased with age. Given that cross-race friendships decrease with age (Aboud, in press) and yet serve as one of the most significant predictors of prejudice reduction (Pettigrew & Tropp, 2000), the use of personal choice to condone exclusion based on race in the friendship context may have negative repercussions on intergroup relationships in late childhood and adulthood. Exploring the extent to which children hold implicit biases about cross-race relationships may shed light on this issue.

Children's reasons for exclusion from the peer group context (music club) included group functioning and, to a lesser extent, group identity. This was consistent with our past studies on children's evaluations of exclusion from peer groups such as ballet, baseball, basketball, and math clubs (Killen & Stangor, 2001). As peer groups increase in importance in development, inclusion and exclusion become salient aspects of social development. Exclusion occurs for a wide range of reasons, and included in this category is maintenance of the group. Only a minority of children and adolescents used explicit stereotypes to justify exclusion in the peer group context. Typically children gave reasons such as "Boys will feel uncomfortable with a girl in the club and they talk about different things" or "Kevin (a Black child) probably doesn't listen to the same kind of music as the others in the club." Again, it is not clear to what extent children are aware that they hold assumptions about what makes a group work well and whether these assumptions actually derive from their experience. Social networks are complex in children's lives (Rubin et al., 1998), and the ways in which networks perpetuate or discourage exclusion based on group membership need to be further studied.

In this project we documented the existence of group functioning as a key aspect of how adolescents evaluate exclusion from groups, and the next step is to determine when this type of reasoning is used by individuals to make decisions about group inclusion. Horn (in press) found that adolescents who condoned exclusion from social reference groups (such as the cheerleaders and the gothics) also used group functioning to justify their decision to exclude. As was found in this study, the majority of students in Horn's study rejected exclusion, and the minority of students who did condone exclusion also used reasons based on group functioning and group identity.

The findings for the school context provided an interesting contrast to the friendship and peer group contexts. Whereas exclusion was rejected by three-fourths (78%) of the participants in the latter two contexts, exclusion was rejected by virtually all of the participants (98%) in the school context. Students stated that it would be wrong for a town to exclude girls or African-American children from attending school and gave moral reasons for their answers. Interestingly, fairness reasoning in this context increased with age. Thus, although adolescents become more likely to justify exclusion in friendship and peer group contexts with age, they also become less likely to justify societally based exclusion. Adolescents who evaluate exclusion in friendship and peer group contexts as all right using personal or social conventional reasons also evaluate exclusion as wrong in the school context using moral reasons; these forms of reasoning co-exist in 10th graders' perspective of exclusion. Even though stereotypes and biases may influence their evaluation of peer group exclusion, these biases are not extended to larger societal contexts such as school.

Exclusion based on gender or race was viewed as wrong by the majority of our participants, and both children and adolescents made distinctions between these two forms of exclusion. Theoretically, gender and racial prejudice are quite different, and there has been extensive analysis on the implications of these different forms of stereotyping. As Aboud and Amato (2001) pointed out, with development, males and females eventually become interdependent through intimate relationships, marriage, and families. This is not the case with individuals from different racial and ethnic backgrounds. In fact, with development, there seems to be increasing segregation and distance given the findings that cross-race friendships decrease with age (Aboud et al., in press). The long-term implications of exclusion based on race, then, may be quite severe (see Opotow, 1990). At the same time, exclusion based on gender has negative long-term consequences in that inequality in the home, particularly in terms of fairness issues and division of labor, can have adverse effects on the socialization of values of equality in children (Nussbaum, 1999; Okin, 1989).

Why do children judge that gender exclusion is more legitimate than exclusion based on race? Social and cultural expectations about gender typically focus on differential social roles in society (e.g., girls should prepare for motherhood, boys for careers). This is much less the case with expectations about race, particularly in the past 50 years (though historically race was tied to social roles, especially in the United States). As Dovidio and Gaertner (2000) have reported, explicit racism has decreased dramatically over the past several decades even though implicit racism, often referred to as subconscious racism, is still fairly pervasive. Current cultural expectations readily exist about the necessity for gender segregation, and much less so for racial segregation.

Moreover, gender segregation is very common on playgrounds and in classrooms in the elementary school years (Maccoby, 2000), and is often a product of socialization and authority sanctions (Bigler et al., 1997). In fact, Bigler (1995) has documented the extensive means by which teachers and individuals in positions of authority encourage gender segregation in the classroom context (e.g., "Line up for recess, girls first, then boys"). By middle school and high school, dating and intimate relationships emerge and dramatically change the dynamics of cross-gender interaction. These developmental changes in cross-gender social relationships may account for some of our findings regarding age-related changes regarding exclusion judgments based on gender and race.

The findings regarding children's evaluations of social influence, authority, and generalizability lead us to conclude that exclusion is a multifaceted phenomenon as defined by social-cognitive domain theory. These assessments have been used in past research to determine when children view a transgression as moral or social-conventional (see Smetana, 1995, for a review). In the present study, the school context was treated as a prototypic moral transgression. Similar to how children judge "hitting someone for no reason" (prototypic moral transgression), the vast majority of participants judged that excluding girls or Black children from school is wrong and should not be allowed even if there is strong social pressure to do so (social consensus), or if the authority mandates it (authority influence), or if it occurs in another country (generalizability). Students' responses to the external sources of influence for the friendship and peer group contexts were different, however, from those for the school context. Social consensus to exclude a peer as a friend because of his or her group membership was a factor for about one-quarter of the participants, and the authority influence was a bit higher, indicating that these forms of nonmoral influence contribute to how children define friendship and peer-group exclusion. A significant minority also viewed exclusion in another country as legitimate due to different customs and social tradition, which reveals that children do not necessarily generalize the wrongfulness of exclusion to other cultural contexts (unlike prototypic moral transgressions, which are viewed as wrong, even in another country).

These results contribute to the social-cognitive domain model by demonstrating that children use different domains of reasoning to evaluate a complex social issue like exclusion (see Turiel, 1983, 1998; Turiel et al., 1987). This supports our theoretical model, which predicted that children's reasoning about complex issues is not "premoral" as theorized by Piaget (1932) and Kohlberg (1969). Piaget predicted that children used premoral reasons, such as authority, to evaluate acts as right or wrong, and Kolhberg theorized that children resorted to punishment avoidance to determine the legitimacy of an act or transgression. To some extent, our findings are more challenging for a Kohlbergian view than a Piagetian view given the age group in our study. Piaget predicted that by 4th grade children would focus on fairness to evaluate interindividual treatment. And, in fact, the children in our study used fairness reasoning in rather dramatic ways as evidenced by the protocol excerpts we reported in the Results section (Chapter IV). The findings are a more direct counter to Kohlberg's theory because he predicted that children do not refer to generalized moral principles until early adolescence. Kohlberg contended that prior to adolescence children evaluate issues as wrong due to punishment avoidance, social roles, laws and regulations, and cultural expectations. In our study, however, 4th, 7th, and 10th graders very clearly rejected social consensus, authority, and cultural expectations when evaluating exclusion based on gender or race. Their reasons were based on unfairness, the wrongfulness of discrimination, and the unequal opportunities that result in discrimination. Further, some children articulated theories about integration, and the need for individuals to learn to get along with people who are different from themselves for the benefit of humanity. For example, one African-American 4th-grade female said:

> It's not okay (for Jerry not to be friends with Damon because he's Black). *Why not?* That makes me think of history. *Why?* Because in Martin Luther King times, Blacks would have to drink at the Black water fountain and Whites would have to drink at the White water fountain. They go to different schools everyplace. It was unfair. And now that the world has changed, Blacks and Whites can play together. If they become friends they will learn to live with each other.

A 10th-grade African-American female stated that: "We need to change our opinions about other people, we need to stop the discrimination. I know it's a hard process, we need to do everything in our power to change it." Children addressed the implications of the cross-race friendship decision beyond their own group, culture, and interpersonal situation.

Not only did children articulate these viewpoints but they also were not easily influenced by interviewer probes in which social influence or authority mandates were reinforced. Researchers in the cognitive area have argued that young children are highly suggestible and particularly so to adult probes (e.g., Ackil & Zaragoza, 1995; Winer & McGlone, 1993). When we used counterprobes to challenge children's initial assertions, children were only influenced by inclusion, not exclusion, considerations. That is, children who had decided it was wrong to exclude someone because of their race or gender did not change their judgment even when a recommendation to exclude was presented. Yet, children who had decided it was all right to exclude someone, frequently changed their judgment after hearing an inclusion suggestion from friends or parents (who said that it would be wrong to exclude). These findings are consistent with results from a prior study we conducted with preschool-aged children in which fairness probes were more effective than were probes about stereotypic expectations regarding gender inclusion choices (see Killen et al., 2001). Our interpretation of this finding is that when children have a chance to explicitly weigh all considerations, fairness takes priority over other concerns such as group functioning and personal choice. This project extends the earlier study by demonstrating a similar effect for older children, with a wider range of contexts, and the application to racial exclusion as well as to gender exclusion.

We did not find that counterprobes were more influential for younger than older children, nor did the gender or ethnicity of the participant make a difference. What we did find was that the positive form of the social consensus probe (that it is wrong to exclude) was more effective than the authority influence probe. These findings tell us that children are critically evaluating suggestions from adult interviewers; they are not persuaded to change their view as a result of just *any* form of suggestion. We interviewed children about peer exclusion in non-school-related contexts, and it was peer influence that had the most positive effect for changing judgments. Authority pressure was less directly influential. This supports a differentiated conception of authority in childhood (see Laupa, 1986). Perhaps children would be more influenced by authority suggestions in contexts in which exclusion is initiated by authority figures or in which authority figures are directly affected by the exclusion. This line of research could provide additional insight into the role of authority on decisions about exclusion.

Our findings regarding the way that participants' grade, gender, and ethnicity influence children's judgments revealed some surprises. First, there were fewer gender and ethnicity findings than we predicted. Most of our findings pertained to age-related (grade) changes. The lack of overall gender findings is in contrast to all of our previous studies on exclusion, which were conducted with predominantly European-American samples, and in which we had demonstrated that girls judge exclusion to be more wrong than do boys (Killen & Stangor, 2001). We interpreted our prior findings of girls' sensitivity to exclusion as due, in part, to their past experience with exclusion, such as in the realm of sports, rather than solely to being female. This led us to predict that minority students (boys and girls) would evaluate exclusion in ways more similar to European-American females than to European-American males given the likelihood that minority students in the United States have also experienced exclusion in one form or another.

To some extent, the lack of gender differences in our results supports our theory about prior experience with exclusion because there were fewer gender differences with this mixed ethnicity sample in contrast to our prior findings with homogeneous European-American samples. This inference has to be taken with caution, however, because we used a different measure of exclusion in this study than in our past studies (and European-American boys did not differ significantly from other groups in this study). One major difference between this study and our prior studies was that in previous studies we assessed how students evaluated exclusion in the context of gender-stereotypic and racial-stereotypic peer activities, such as excluding girls from baseball, boys from ballet, or Black children from math clubs and White children from basketball teams. In the present study, we purposefully chose nonstereotypic contexts to determine whether negative judgments about exclusion would be applied to nonstereotypic situations. Research has shown stronger stereotypic preferences for boys than for girls (Ruble & Martin, 1998), a finding that may have contributed to the greater gender differences in stereotypic contexts in our previous studies than were found in the nonstereotypic contexts used in this study. It could be that greater gender differences emerge when children are asked about exclusion in stereotypic contexts (girls from baseball, boys from ballet) than when they are asked about exclusion from nonstereotypic contexts (such as friendship or a music club).

Nonetheless, we found several gender findings that reflected previously reported gender patterns, which indicated to us that further research should directly examine this issue. First, a significant percentage of boys used group functioning to evaluate gender exclusion in the peer group music club context—more so than did girls. Second, boys were more likely than girls to condone the exclusion of girls from a music club in another cultural context, and to use reasons based on personal choice and social tradition when making these judgments. Third, adolescent boys were more likely than younger boys to view gender exclusion in the friendship context as a personal decision, and were more likely than girls to view racial exclusion in the friendship context as a personal decision. Fourth, adolescent European-American boys used less fairness reasoning than did adolescent minority boys when evaluating exclusion based on gender in the friendship context. Finally, girls changed in the positive direction as a result of external influence probes more than did boys (and minority participants did so more than nonminority participants). Taken together, these findings indicate that *in some contexts* boys evaluate exclusion as a personal decision or as a matter of group functioning more often than do girls.

The fact that there were few differences between European-American males and minority males may be due to the ceiling effect for racial exclusion in this study. Virtually all students rejected racial exclusion. Given that exclusion was only condoned in the gender context may have contributed to the lack of minority-nonminority differences for the evaluation of exclusion. Future studies testing implicit biases about racial exclusion may reveal more complex gender-by-ethnicity patterns of judgments than were found in this study.

Generally, we expected more diversity in evaluations of exclusion from participants in the four ethnic groups we interviewed in this study. There were few overall differences based on the ethnicity of the participants. There were no main effects regarding ethnicity for whether children judged exclusion to be all right or not all right. As predicted, however, there were differences in the types of reasoning (justifications) that minority children used in contrast to those used by European-American children. African-American children were more likely to use reasons based on empathy and to comment about negative consequences to society when individuals discriminate on the basis of race (referred to as *integration justifications*) than were European-American children. Integration was coded when the participants' reasons about the wrongfulness of exclusion went beyond the situation being evaluated and referred to the negative consequences that result when individuals exclude others on the basis of skin color. For example, when evaluating a boy's decision not to be friends with a Black child, African-Americans spoke about the need for individuals from different backgrounds to learn to live together and the negative consequences for a society in which individuals practice discrimination based on race. European-American students who said exclusion was wrong because it was unfair or involved unequal treatment were less likely to refer to the larger societal problems that exist when individuals use race as a reason for exclusion. When rejecting social consensus, African-American 4th graders used empathy more often than did European-American 4th graders: "Think how she would feel if they didn't let her in the club. She would feel very bad."

These findings confirmed our expectation that, in some cases, African-American children would express a greater sensitivity to the wrongfulness of exclusion than would European-American children. We use the term *sensitivity* to convey the sense that African-Americans' reactions to exclusion are deeply felt and widely experienced. There were no differences in the moral evaluations of the wrongfulness of exclusion in this study between students from diverse ethnic backgrounds. European-American children viewed it as wrong and used reasons based on fairness and unequal treatment. Minority children used fairness and unequal treatment as well and, in addition, they talked about how the excluded child would feel and the negative consequences to society when individuals use race as a reason for friendship and peer club membership. These justifications (empathy and integration) reflected a small proportion of the overall use of moral reasons and it would be helpful to know more about the contexts in which children use these types of reasons and whether the tendency to use these types of reasons are predictive of social or school adjustment. In future research it would be fruitful to analyze children's direct experience with exclusion as well as their ethnic identity in order to further understand children's exclusion judgments. Researchers who study ethnic identity (Phinney, 1990; Phinney et al., 1997) have demonstrated that ethnic identity is related to self-esteem and school adjustment, particularly in adolescence. Thus, ethnic identity may be related to the likelihood of using more generalized statements about the wrongfulness of exclusion; this remains to be investigated.

The only significant differences between the African-American, Latin-American, and Asian-American students were revealed in their evaluations of authority influence on exclusion, and the extent to which they switched their judgments as a function of the external influence probes. When evaluating exclusion from the peer group, Latin-American and Asian-American students referred to authority jurisdiction more often than did African-American students. In addition, Latin-American and Asian-American students changed in a positive direction for all three external influence probes (social consensus, authority, and generalizability) more often than did African-American students. These findings indicate that the social influence (of peers and authority) provided a more salient consideration for Latin-American and Asian-American students when evaluating exclusion than for African-American and European-American students. Perhaps the "outsider" perspective on the scenarios prompted Latin-American and Asian-American students to be more willing to change their judgments when contemplating another perspective. Minority groups experience very different forms of exclusion in the United States based on complex political and historical patterns (Demo & Hughes, 1990; Fischer & Shaw, 1999; Ogbu, 1994) and these issues need to be incorporated into studies of children's evaluations of exclusion. Future research on social and ethnic identity as well as exclusion of individuals from a wider range of ethnic backgrounds will lead to better understanding of these findings.

There were several gender differences within the African-American sample, particularly in adolescence. Among African-American 10th graders, females used more fairness than did males when evaluating a club's decision to exclude a girl. When evaluating the school context, African-American 10th-grade females evaluated exclusion as more wrong than did African-American 10th-grade males. Thus, adolescent African-American females were more likely to view exclusion as wrong for fairness reasons than were African-American males. African-American adolescent males are continually confronted with negative messages about the treatment of females (e.g., in rap music and videos), and this media image has raised concerns about African-American male viewpoints on gender equality. Several of our findings reflected a negative viewpoint about African-American boys' evaluations of gender exclusion in contrast to African-American girls' evaluations. Yet, the majority of our findings pointed to African-American males' rejection of gender exclusion (using reasons based on unfairness and unequal treatment). Going against stereotypic expectations, then, we found that most African-American males did not evaluate gender or racial exclusion differently from females or participants from other ethnic backgrounds. As we discuss below, the participants in our sample were from middle-class and working-class backgrounds and were not from high stress, inner-city environments, and this may contribute to our positive findings. At the same time, research has shown that young African-American men experience considerable racial discrimination, which contributes to their degraded status in U.S. culture (Gary, 1995). Moreover, Fisher and colleagues (2000) found that half of the African-American males they surveyed reported being harassed by store clerks and viewed as dangerous in institutional settings. Thus, African-American males experience rejection based, in their view, solely on the color of their skin. This past experience with exclusion, as well as their degraded status, may result in a mixture of judgments by African-American males. On the one hand, their past experience with exclusion makes them more aware of the wrongfulness of it; on the other hand, their degraded status may create an identification with the victimizer in adolescence, as has been documented by Graham and Juvonen (1998). Clearly, more research needs to be conducted in this area.

Given that intimacy manifests in adolescence (Laursen & Williams, 1997; Shulman & Scharf, 2000) it is also feasible that the dating factor entered into adolescent boys' judgments about exclusion of a girl in the friendship context This supports a recent study conducted with college students in which the decision to refrain from dating someone of another race was viewed as legitimate because it was a personal decision in contrast to other cross-race decisions, such as voting for someone because of their race, which were viewed as wrong and unfair (Killen et al., 2002). Adolescents may view gender exclusion as a matter of personal choice in the way that decisions about dating are viewed as a matter of personal choice; in general, intimacy is viewed as a personal decision by adolescents. Yet, girls, who were the targets of exclusion, did not view gender exclusion in these terms but as a matter of unfairness or discrimination. Thus, even though the dating factor may have emerged for boys, girls at the same age viewed exclusion from a friendship or a peer group perspective and evaluated it as wrong in moral terms, not as legitimate for personal reasons.

The gender and ethnicity findings intersected with our age-related findings because the most predominant age-related pattern was the increase in the use of social-conventional and personal reasons for justifying exclusion with age. To some extent this maps onto the age-related reports of peer rejection. Graham and Juvonen (1998), in their review of the literature on peer rejection and aggression, discussed how the relationship between rejection and aggression changes in adolescence. During adolescence, there is a short-lived period in which students identify with individuals who demonstrate deviant behavior, such as relational aggression and the exclusion of others (see also Moffitt, 1993). This may explain why African-American males judged exclusion of a Black child from a peer group as more all right than did Latin-American and Asian-American students.

94

We view this connection with caution because there is no clear evidence, so far, that condoning exclusion reflects a negative intention to harm another. There are many societal instances in which exclusion, for example based on gender, is condoned and justified as a means to make a group function well (e.g., same-sex schools, Boy Scouts, fraternities and sororities), and in which decisions about friendship are viewed as personal decisions. Further, there were also age-related patterns in which exclusion was viewed as increasingly wrong with age, such as in the response to authority mandates. When considering why it would be wrong to exclude a Black child from a music club even if the parents said it was all right to do so, adolescents used more reasons based on fairness than did 4th graders (younger children used more reasons based on empathy than did older children). There may be some times in which these decisions are motivated by stereotypes, and research needs to be conducted to determine when supporting exclusion is, in fact, a cover for stereotypic thinking or prejudicial attitudes.

In general, the age-related findings revealed that 10th-grade adolescents judge it more all right to exclude someone from a friendship relationship or a peer group than do younger children. As predicted, the most striking findings were shown for the peer group context in which 10th graders were more likely to judge excluding a girl or a Black child from a music club as legitimate. As mentioned earlier, these judgments were based on personal choice reasons, which included personal prerogatives and preference, as well as social group functioning justifications, which included group identity, customs, and traditions. Very few adolescents referred to peer influence as a reason for their decision; rather it was a matter of autonomy and what makes a group function well. In fact, 10th graders were most likely to explicitly reject social consensus as a reason to exclude someone, referring to independent decision-making by the group as central to their decision ("They shouldn't be influenced by what others tell them to do"). This was particularly true when the authority influence probes were introduced. Adolescents rejected parental and governmental authority viewpoints condoning exclusion, unlike younger children who were sometimes swayed by the authority influence.

Yet, 10th-grade adolescents did not generalize their judgments about the wrongfulness of exclusion to other cultural contexts to the same extent as did younger children. In some cases 10th graders condoned the exclusion of a friend or a member of a group (based on gender or race) in another country indicating that social traditions and customs were important, and in other cases 10th graders applied their fairness reasoning to exclusion based on race in another country more than did younger children.

The overall picture of the age-related changes indicates that adolescents have a more differentiated view about exclusion than do younger children, and that they are more likely to view exclusion in terms of morality, autonomy, and social-conventional considerations. On the one side, this is consistent with prior findings on the increase in adolescents' application of a wide range of reasons for understanding complex social interactions (Smetana, 1988; Turiel, 1983). On the other hand, this may also reflect an increase in the desire to conform to groups (Berndt, 1992; Brown, Eicher, & Petrie, 1986) even at the cost of condoning discriminatory behavior. Investigating adolescents' reasoning about exclusion in other social contexts, aside from the ones described in this study, will provide a more comprehensive viewpoint of their social judgments about exclusion.

In future research, it would be helpful to further explore children's conceptions of equal opportunity, equal treatment, and fairness considerations in the context of exclusion and inclusion. Roemer (1998), a political scientist, philosopher, and economist, delineated two conceptions of equality of opportunity prevalent in modern democracies. The first theory recommends that cultures should "level the playing field" and do what it can to help individuals compete for positions, "or more generally, . . . level the playing field among individuals during their periods of formation, so that all those with relevant potential will eventually be admissible to pools of candidates competing for positions" (p. 1). The second theory is the nondiscrimination principle, which states that individuals should only be evaluated by the attributes that are tied to the performance of a task or duty in question. In this theory, categories of gender and race should not enter the judgment. Roemer argued that the nondiscrimination principle derives from the level-the-playing-field principle. His analysis of these theories involves a proposal for a precise way to organize these diverse conceptions. He generates formal (mathematical) formulas to determine how one should calculate the variables that are necessary to determine how one should level the playing field in different areas such as equal opportunity of production, welfare, and health.

What makes this work relevant for our developmental analyses is that Roemer provides conceptual distinctions between different types of equal opportunity types of judgments. To date, no developmental work has sought to determine what types of equal opportunity judgments children understand or use when evaluating exclusion and this would be a productive line of research to pursue. For example, some children state that the peer group should admit girls "so that girls can learn more about CDs, too." In this case there seems to be an assumption that inclusion is necessary to level the playing field—that is, to give girls opportunities to learn the things boys know so that girls will be prepared for future opportunities. This type of judgment was quite pervasive in several previous studies in which we asked children to pick one of two children for a club that was traditionally stereotypic (ballet, baseball) (Killen & Stangor, 2001). Many children gave responses such as "I would pick the girl for baseball because if she learns more about it then maybe more girls will play and they will get to play in the majors, too". For the most part, we categorized children's judgments about equal opportunity, equality, and fairness in one category ("moral") and it would be fruitful to evaluate children's differentiated understanding of these principles in the context of decision-making that involves stereotypic expectations.

Along the same lines, more research is necessary to differentiate chil-dren' various subtypes of social-conventional reasoning. This includes their judgments about group functioning, group identity, stereotypes, and shared beliefs. In particular, more research is needed to disentangle children's judgments about group functioning from their implicit or explicit use of stereotypes. One way to do this would be to design studies that assess children's implicit use of stereotypes, and to determine whether this type of implicit knowledge bears on more explicit decision-making about ex-clusion and inclusion. For example, when children state that it is all right to exclude someone from the peer group because they "don't share the same interests," what underlies the assumption of nonshared interests? Is it based solely on skin color? How aware are children that they are attrib-uting a trait to an individual based solely on group membership? Social psychologists have conducted extensive studies with adults on implicit bi-ases and racism (see Dovidio et al., 2000; Gaertner & Dovidio, 1986). Very little research on implicit biases has been conducted with children (see Hirschfeld, 1995; Sagar & Schofield, 1980). These aspects of exclu-sion and inclusion decisions require further systematic and empirical investigation.

What are the implications for children's social development when ex-clusion occurs based on group membership? Researchers studying preju-dice and stereotyping have pointed to a number of negative consequences of this type of exclusion (Aboud & Amato, 2001; Aboud & Levy, 2000; Sears & Levy, in press). Children who experience prejudice and stereo-typing from their peers are at risk for developing negative self-esteem as well as for doing poorly in school contexts. Steele (1997) and Steele and Aronson (1995) have shown that the threat of a stereotype systematically affects how students perform in class and on academic measurements of achievement. For example, students who are explicitly made aware of stereo-types about their gender or race group membership perform worse on classroom tests than do students (at the same level of pretest ability) who are not explicitly directed to think about stereotypes (Aronson, 2002). Although little is known about the long-term consequences of peer prejudice and stereotyping, exclusionary attitudes reinforce the notion of differential treatment on the basis of group membership. Moreover, most forms of exclusion are undesirable from the viewpoint of the targets of exclusion.

Being excluded from groups because of one's gender or race has the potential to lead to peer harassment and victimization, although no studies that we know of have investigated this connection in childhood. Most of the literature on peer victimization and peer harassment has focused on school bullying and the social-cognitive correlates of peer aggression (Graham & Juvonen, 1998, 2001; Graham & Taylor, 2002; Hawker & Boulton, 2000; Kochenderfer-Ladd & Ladd, 2001; Olweus, 1993; Rubin et al., 1998). For example, it is well documented that aggressive boys often infer hostile intent on the part of their peers, particularly in ambiguous provocative situations (see Crick & Dodge, 1994). Graham and Juvonen (1998) analyzed the findings in the peer aggression and peer victimization literatures to demonstrate that aggressive children and victimized children hold biases about peers that have different long-term implications.

Most centrally, the findings indicate that there are long-term negative consequences for both aggressive children (rejection from peers, low self-esteem) and victimized children (anxiety, loneliness, and aversion to school). Very little of this research, however, has examined whether victimization occurs because of prejudice and stereotypes. Instead, the focus has been on the social-cognitive attributions of the individual child as well as the individual child's social deficits (see Graham & Juvonen, 1998). It would be fruitful to draw on these two diverse areas of research to determine whether children who readily exclude others based on group membership also victimize other children based on group membership; further, children who experience exclusion based on group membership may also experience victimization. Arsenio and Lemerise (2001) have pointed to ways in which research on children's social and moral judgments are informative about children's attributions of their peers' intentions, particularly in the areas of aggression.

Our contention at the outset of this *Monograph* that peer rejection needs to be examined from a social group process model is warranted based on our findings. Peer rejection, which is a widely studied phenomenon (Asher & Coie, 1991; Rubin et al., 1998), is not solely the result of the social deficits of the individual. There are times when individuals are rejected for reasons that have nothing to do with their social inadequacies. Instead, rejection from a relationship or a social group may be based solely on one's group membership, such as gender or race. Children articulated this viewpoint in interviews, indicating that it is highly likely that this actually happens in their peer social interactions. Though we did not focus on individual differences, we did find a small minority of participants who condoned exclusion across a range of contexts and used much less moral reasoning than most of the participants in the study. Identifying these children and expanding the range of assessments regarding their evaluation of exclusion would provide a window into the developmental origins of individuals who are at risk for extreme exclusionary behavior as studied by Opotow (1990) and Staub (1990).

A next step for this line of work is to examine the role that children's social experience plays in how children make judgments about exclusion (see Killen, Crystal, & Ruck, 2002). In the present study we interviewed children living in a middle- and working-class, mixed-ethnicity school district. Participants interacted with peers from a wide range of cultural and ethnic backgrounds. As one African-American adolescent put it, "I live with Cambodians, Ethiopians, and Asians, all kinds of people, and everyone has a heart." This may account, in part, for the high level of sensitivity, or judgments about the wrongfulness of exclusion in our samples, across all participants. This would be consistent with Pettigrew's (1998) theory that under certain conditions, intergroup contact can reduce prejudice and discrimination (see also Pettigrew & Tropp, 2000). The assessments used in this study need to be applied to students from both the majority and minority cultures attending homogenous schools. For example, do European-American students attending schools that are 100% European-American differ from European-American students attending mixed-ethnicity schools in how they evaluate exclusion? Similarly, do African-American and other minority students' evaluations of exclusion vary as a function of attending homogeneous or heterogeneous schools? Intergroup contact alone is not enough to facilitate positive intergroup attitudes, however. In school settings, it is important to examine the messages from authority figures, the nature of intergroup interactions (competitive or cooperative), the presence of common goals, and the opportunities for personalized interactions (Pettigrew & Tropp, 2001).

An additional line of inquiry that would complement analyses of children's and adolescents' school environments has to do with family and parental influence. What messages do parents transmit regarding inclusion and exclusion of others? How do children evaluate these messages? Though the family is only one source of influence (see Aboud & Amato, 2001), it is necessary to understand how children evaluate parental expectations and the ways in which parental styles of interactions with children promote or inhibit a social awareness about exclusion (based on gender or race). This study investigated developmental changes that occur regarding social reasoning about exclusion.

Further, we need to better understand the complex relationship between gender and ethnicity. Does the wrongfulness of exclusion based on race transfer to decisions about the wrongfulness of exclusion based on gender? Does intergroup contact regarding ethnicity provide experiences relevant to reasoning about exclusion based on gender or is this type of experience specifically tied to reasoning about race and ethnicity? At times, participants in this study viewed gender exclusion as legitimate (from a group functioning or personal choice perspective) and racial exclusion as wrong (from a fairness standpoint). What types of social experiences account for these different judgments and reasons? Are these forms of exclusion different due to different histories and consequences or is it a matter of social experience and societal expectations? We did not test these hypotheses in this study and the connection between different sources of experience and reasoning about varied forms of exclusion needs to be better understood. Thus, studies designed to examine social experience need to incorporate assessments regarding school environment, intergroup friendships, social identity, and past experience with exclusion in order to explain why some children view certain forms of exclusion as more wrong than other forms of exclusion.

Our findings revealed that, on the one hand, children and adolescents from four different ethnic backgrounds viewed exclusion based on group membership as wrong, and, on the other hand, there were differences in evaluations of exclusion as a function of the context and the target of exclusion, as well as the age, gender, and ethnicity of the participants. The results support our theoretical model of exclusion, which proposes that multiple forms of reasoning are brought to bear on decisions about exclusion. Understanding how children and adolescents make these types of judgments provides a window into how individuals make complex decisions, ones that involve weighing group functioning and personal choice with justice, fairness, and equal treatment for all.

SCENARIOS AND QUESTIONS USED IN THE INTERVIEW

FRIENDSHIP CONTEXT

Gender Target

Tom lives on Park Street. Sally moves in next door. She wants to make new friends, so she goes next door and asks Tom if he wants to hang out. Tom doesn't want to hang out with Sally because she is a girl.

Q1. Evaluation: Do you think it's okay for Tom to not hang out with Sally because she is a girl?

Q2. Justification: *Why do you think it is okay/not okay?*

For a Judgment of Not Okay

Q3N. Social influence: *What if Tom's friends say that they don't think he should hang out with Sally because she's a girl. Do you think it's okay, then?*

Q4N. Justification: *Why?*

Q5N. Authority: *What if Tom's parents say it's okay for Tom to not hang out with Sally because she's a girl. Do you think it's okay, then?*

Q6N. Justification: *Why?*

Q7N. Generalizability: *What about in another country, would it be okay for a boy who lives there to not hang out with someone because she's a girl?*

Q8N. Justification: *Why?*

For a Judgment of Okay

Q3A. Social influence: *What if Tom's friends say that they think he should hang out with Sally even though she's a girl? Do you think it's okay, then?*

Q4A. Justification: *Why?*

Q5A. Authority: *What if Tom's parents say that he should hang out with Sally even though she's a girl. Do you think it's okay, then?*

Q6A. Justification: *Why?*

Q7A. Generalizability: *What about in another country, would it be okay for a boy who lives there to not hang out with someone because she's a girl?*

Q8A. Justification: *Why?*

Race Target

Jerry, who is White, lives on Maple Street. Damon moves in next door. He wants to make new friends, so he goes next door and asks Jerry if he wants to hang out. Jerry doesn't want to hang out with Damon because he's Black.

Q1. Evaluation: *Do you think it's okay for Jerry to not hang out with Damon because he is Black?*

Q2. Justification: *Why do you think it is okay/not okay?*

For a Judgment of Not Okay

Q3N. Social influence: *What if Jerry's friends say that they don't think he should hang out with Damon because he's Black? Do you think it's okay, then?*

Q4N. Justification: *Why?*

Q5N. Authority: *What if Jerry's parents say it's okay for Jerry to not hang out with Damon because he is Black. Do you think it's okay, then?*

Q6N. Justification: *Why?*

Q7N. Generalizability: *What about in another country, would it be okay for a boy who lives there to not hang out with someone because they're Black?*

Q8N. Justification: *Why?*

For a Judgment of Okay

Q3A. Social influence: *What if Jerry's friends say that they think he should hang out with Damon even though he's Black? Do you think it's okay, then?*

Q4A. Justification: *Why?*

Q5A. Authority: *What if Jerry's parents say that he should hang out with Damon even though he is Black. Do you think it's okay, then?*

Q6A. Justification: *Why?*

Q7A. Generalizability: *What about in another country, would it be okay for a boy who lives there to not hang out with someone because they're Black?*

Q8A. Justification: *Why?*

PEER GROUP CONTEXT

Gender Target

Mike and some of his friends form a music club where they collect and trade CDs. Jessica hears about the club and how much fun they have and wants to join. But Mike and his friends do not let her join because she's a girl. They want to keep the club all boys.

Q1. Evaluation: *Do you think it's okay for Mike and his friends to not let Jessica join their club because she's a girl?*

Q2. Justification: *Why do you think it is okay/not okay?*

For a Judgment of Not Okay

Q3N. Social influence: *What if other kids who want to join the club tell Mike and his friends that they don't think the music club should let Jessica join because she's a girl?*

Q4N. Justification: *Why?*

Q5N. Authority: *What if Mike's parents say that it's okay for the music club to not let Jessica join because she is a girl. Do you think it's okay, then?*

Q6N. Justification: *Why?*

Q7N. Generalizability: *What about in another country, would it be okay for a music club there to not let someone join their club because they're a girl?*

Q8N. Justification: *Why?*

For a Judgment of Okay

Q3A. Social influence: *What if other kids who want to join the club tell Mike and his friends that they think the club should let Jessica join even though she's a girl?*

Q4A. Justification: *Why?*

Q5A. Authority: *What if Mike's parents say that the boys should let Jessica join even though she is a girl. Do you think it's okay, then?*

Q6A. Justification: *Why?*

Q7A. Generalizability: *What about in another country, would it be okay for a music club there to not let someone join their club because they're a girl?*

Q8A. Justification: *Why?*

Race Target

Joe is a White student. Joe and some of his White friends form a music club where they collect and trade CDs. Kevin hears about the club and how much fun they have and wants to join. But Joe and his friends

103

do not let him join because Kevin is Black. They want to keep the club all White so they can have their own club.

Q1. Evaluation: *Do you think it's okay for Joe and his friends to not let Kevin join their club because he is Black?*

Q2. Justification: *Why do you think it is okay/not okay?*

For a Judgment of Not Okay

Q3N. Social influence: *What if other kids who want to join the club tell Joe and his friends that they don't think the club should let Kevin join because he's Black?*

Q4N. *Why?*

Q5N. Authority: *What if Joe's parents say that it's okay for Joe and his friends to not let Kevin join because he is Black. Do you think it's okay, then?*

Q6N. Justification: *Why?*

Q7N. Generalizability: *What about in another country, would it be okay for a White club there to not let someone join their club because they're Black?*

Q8N. Justification: *Why?*

For a Judgment of Okay

Q3A. Social influence: *What if other kids who want to join the club tell Joe and his friends that they think the club should let Kevin join even though he's Black?*

Q4A. Justification: *Why?*

Q5A. Authority: *What if Joe's parents say that they should let Kevin join even though he is Black. Do you think it's okay, then?*

Q6A. Justification: *Why?*

Q7A. Generalizability: *What about in another country, would it be okay for a White club there to not let someone join their club because they're Black?*

Q8A. Justification: *Why?*

SCHOOL CONTEXT

Gender Target

There is a town that doesn't let girls go to school because that's the way it's always been. Amy really wants to go to school but she isn't allowed to go because she is a girl.

Q1. Evaluation: *Do you think it's okay for Amy to not be allowed to go to school because she is a girl?*

Q2. Justification: *Why do you think it is okay/not okay?*

For a Judgment of Not Okay

Q3N. Social influence: *What if the people in the town say that they don't think Amy should be allowed to go to school because she's a girl? Do you think it's okay, then?*

Q4N. Justification: *Why?*

Q5N. Authority: *What if the government says that it's okay for the town to not let Amy to go to school because she is a girl. Do you think it's okay, then?*

Q6N. Justification: *Why?*

Q7N. Generalizability: *What about in another country, would it be okay for a town there to not let someone go to school because they're a girl?*

Q8N. Justification: *Why?*

For a judgment of Okay

Q3A. Social influence: *What if the people in the town say that they think Amy should be allowed to go to school even though she's a girl? Do you think it's okay, then?*

Q4A. Justification: *Why?*

Q5A. Authority: *What if the government says that the town should let Amy to go to school even though she is a girl. Do you think it is okay, then?*

Q6A. Justification: *Why?*

Q7A. Generalizability: *What about in another country, would it be okay for a town there to not let someone go to school because they're a girl?*

Q8A. Justification: *Why?*

Race Target

There is a town that doesn't let Black children go to school because that's the way it's always been. Tony really wants to go to school but he isn't allowed to go because he is Black.

Q1. Evaluation: *Do you think it's okay for Tony to not be allowed to go to school because he's Black?*

Q2 . Justification: *Why do you think it is okay/not okay?*

For a Judgment of Not Okay

Q3N. Social influence: *What if the people in the town say that they don't think Tony should be allowed to go to school because he's Black? Do you think it's okay, then?*

Q4N. Justification: *Why?*

Q5N. Authority: *What if the government says it's okay for the town to not let Tony to go to school because he's Black. Do you think it's okay, then?*

Q6N. Justification: *Why?*

Q7N. Generalizability: *What about in another country, would it be okay for a town there to not let someone go to school because they're Black?*

Q8N. Justification: *Why?*

For a Judgment of Okay

Q3A. Social influence: *What if the people in the town say that they think Tony should be allowed to go to school even though he's Black? Do you think it's okay, then?*

Q4A. Justification: *Why?*

Q5A. Authority: *What if the government says that the town should let Tony to go to school even though he is Black. Do you think it is okay, then?*

Q6A. Justification: *Why?*

Q7A. Generalizability: *What about in another country, would it be okay for a town there to not let someone go to school because they're Black?*

Q8A. Justification: *Why?*

The protocol is designed as follows: context by target of exclusion by evaluation assessment question by justification probe. The scenarios were counterbalanced by context; the target and order of questions were the same.

I. FRIENDSHIP CONTEXT
   A. Target of exclusion: Gender
      1. Evaluation: *All right to exclude? Why?*
      2. Social influence? *Why?*
      3. Authority jurisdiction? *Why?*
      4. Generalizability? *Why?*
   B. Target of exclusion: Race
      5. Evaluation: *All right to exclude? Why?*
      6. Social influence? *Why?*
      7. Authority jurisdiction? *Why?*
      8. Generalizability? *Why?*

II. PEER GROUP CONTEXT
   A. Target of exclusion: Gender
      9. Evaluation: *All right to exclude? Why?*
      10. Social influence? *Why?*
      11. Authority jurisdiction? *Why?*
      12. Generalizability? *Why?*
   B. Target of exclusion: Race
      13. Evaluation: *All right to exclude? Why?*
      14. Social influence? *Why?*
      15. Authority jurisdiction? *Why?*
      16. Generalizability? *Why?*

III. SCHOOL CONTEXT
    A. Target of exclusion: Gender
        17. Evaluation: *All right to exclude? Why?*
        18. Social Influence? *Why?*
        19. Authority jurisdiction? *Why?*
        20. Generalizability? *Why?*
    B. Target of exclusion: Race
        21. Evaluation: *All right to exclude? Why?*
        22. Social influence? *Why?*
        23. Authority Jurisdiction? *Why?*
        24. Generalizability? *Why?*

REFERENCES

Aboud, F. E. (1988). *Children and prejudice.* New York: Basil Blackwell.

Aboud, F. E. (1992). Conflict and group relations. In C. U. Shantz & W. W. Hartup (Eds.), *Conflict in child and adolescent development.* Cambridge, England: Cambridge University Press.

Aboud, F. E. (in press). The formation of ingroup favoritism and outgroup prejudice in young children: Are they distinct attitudes? *Developmental Psychology.*

Aboud, F. E., & Amato, M. (2001). Developmental and socialization influences on intergroup bias. In R. Brown & S. Gaertner (Eds.), *Blackwell handbook of social psychology: Intergroup processes.* Oxford, England: Blackwell Publishers.

Aboud, F. E., & Levy, S. (2000). Interventions to reduce prejudice and discrimination in children and adolescents. In S. Oskamp (Ed.), *Reducing prejudice and discrimination.* Mahwah, NJ: Erlbaum.

Aboud, F. E., Mendolsohn, M. J., & Purdy, P. (in press). Cross-race peer relations and friendship quality. *International Journal of Behavioral Development.*

Ackil, J. K., & Zaragoza, M. S. (1995). Developmental differences in eyewitness suggestibility and memory for source. *Journal of Experimental Child Psychology, 60,* 57–83.

Allport, G. W. (1954). *The nature of prejudice.* Reading, MA: Addison-Wesley.

Ardila-Rey, A., & Killen, M. (2001). Colombian preschool children's judgments about autonomy and conflict resolution in the classroom setting. *International Journal of Behavioral Development, 25*(3), 246–255.

Aronson, J. (Ed.). (2002). *Improving academic achievement: Psychological foundations of education.* San Diego: Academic Press.

Arsenio, W. F., & Fleiss, K. (1996). Typical and behaviorally disruptive children's understanding of the emotional consequences of socio-moral events. *British Journal of Developmental Psychology, 14,* 173–186.

Arsenio, W. F., & Lemerise, E. (2001). Varieties of childhood bullying: Values, emotion processes, and social competence. *Social Development, 10,* 59–73.

Arsenio, W. F., & Lover, A. (1995). Children's conceptions of sociomoral affect: Happy victimizers, mixed, emotions, and other expectancies. In M. Killen & D. Hart (Eds.), *Morality in everyday life: Developmental perspectives.* Cambridge, England: Cambridge University Press.

Asch, S. (1952). *Social psychology.* New York: Prentice-Hall.

Asher, S., & Coie, J. (1990). *Peer rejection in childhood.* Cambridge, England: Cambridge University Press.

Banton, M. (1998). *Racial theories.* Cambridge, England: Cambridge University Press.

Bar-Tal, D. (1996). Development of social categories and stereotypes in early childhood: The case of "the Arab" concept formation, stereotype and attitudes by Jewish children in Israel. *International Journal of Intercultural Relations, 20,* 341–370.

Bennett, M., Barrett, M., Lyons, E., & Sani, F. (1998). Children's subjective identification with the group and ingroup favoritism. *Developmental Psychology*, **34**, 902–909.

Berndt, T. (1992). Friendship and friends' influence in adolescence. *Current Directions in Psychological Science*, **1**, 156–159.

Bigler, R. (1995). The role of classification skill in moderating environmental influences on children's gender stereotyping: A study of the functional use of gender in the classroom. *Child Development*, **66**, 1072–1087.

Bigler, R., Jones, L. C., & Lobliner, D. (1997). Social categorization and the formation of intergroup attitudes in children. *Child Development*, **68**, 530–543.

Bigler, R., & Liben, L. S. (1993). Cognitive mechanisms in children's gender stereotyping: Theoretical and educational implications of a cognitive-based intervention. *Child Development*, **63**, 1351–1363.

Bregman, G., & Killen, M. (1999). Adolescents' and young adults' reasoning about career choice and the role of parental influence. *Journal of Research on Adolescence*, **9**(3), 253–275.

Brewer, M. B. (1979). In-group bias in the minimal intergroup situation: A cognitive-motivational hypothesis. *Psychological Bulletin*, **86**, 307–324.

Brewer, M. B., & Brown, R. (1998). Intergroup relations. In D. Gilbert, S. Fiske, & G. Lindzey (Eds.), *Handbook of social psychology* (Vol. 2). Boston: McGraw-Hill.

Brown, B. (1989). The role of peer groups in adolescent's adjustment to secondary school. In T. Berndt, & G. Ladd (Eds.), *Peer relationships in child development*. New York: Wiley.

Brown, B. B., Eicher, S. A., & Petrie, S. (1986). The importance of peer group ("crowd") affiliation in adolescence. *Journal of Adolescence*, **9**, 73–96.

Brown, R., & Gaertner, S. (2001). *Blackwell handbook of social psychology: Intergroup processes*. Oxford, England: Blackwell Press.

Cairns, E. (1989). Social identity and intergroup conflicts in Northern Ireland: A developmental perspective. In J. Harbison (Ed.), *Growing up in Northern Ireland*. Belfast: Stranmillis College

Carter, D. B., & Patterson, C. J. (1982). Sex roles as social conventions: The development of children's conceptions of sex-role stereotypes. *Developmental Psychology*, **18**, 812–824.

Coie, J. D., & Koeppl, G. K. (1990). Adapting intervention to the problems of aggressive and disruptive rejected children. In S. Asher & J. Coie (Eds.), *Peer rejection in childhood*. New York: Cambridge University Press.

Cole, C., Arafat, C., Tidhar, C., Zidan, W. T., Fox, N. A., Killen, M., Leavitt, L., Lesser, G., Richman, B. A., Ardila-Rey, A., & Yung, F. (in press). The educational impact of Rechov Sumsum/Shara'a Simsim, a television series for Israeli and Palestinian children. *International Journal of Behavioral Development*.

Crick, N. (1997). Engagement in gender normative versus nonnormative forms of aggression: Links to social-psychological adjustment. *Developmental Psychology*, **33**(4), 610–617.

Crick, N., & Dodge, K. (1989). Children's perceptions of peer entry and conflict situations: Social strategies, goals, and outcome expectations. In B. Schneider, J. Nadel, G. Atteli, & R. Weissberg (Eds.), *Social competence in developmental perspective*. Boston: Kluwer.

Crick, N., & Dodge, K. (1994). A review and reformulation of social information-processing mechanisms in children's social adjustment. *Psychological Bulletin*, **115**(1), 74–101.

Crick, N., & Grotpeter, J. (1995). Relational aggression, gender, and social psychological adjustment. *Child Development*, **66**, 710–722.

Crystal, D., Watanabe, H., & Chen, R. (2000). Reactions to morphological deviance: A comparison of Japanese and American children and adolescents. *Social Development*, **9**(1), 40–61.

Damon, W. (1977). *The social world of the child*. San Francisco: Jossey-Bass.

Davidson, P., Turiel, E., & Black, A. (1983). The effect of stimulus familiarity on the use of criteria and justifications in children's social reasoning. *British Journal of Developmental Psychology*, 1, 49–65.

Demo, D. H., & Hughes, M. (1990). Socialization and racial identity among Black Americans. *Social Psychology Quarterly*, 53, 364–374.

Devine, P. G., Plant, E. A., & Buswell, B. N. (2000). Breaking the prejudice habit: Progress and obstacles. In S. Oskamp (Ed.), *Reducing prejudice and discrimination*. Mahwah, NJ: Erlbaum.

Dovidio, J., & Gaertner, S. (2000). Aversive racism and selection decisions. *Psychological Science*, 11(4), 315–319.

Dovidio, J. F., Kawakami, K., & Gaertner, S. L. (2000). Reducing contemporary prejudice: Combating explicit and implicit bias at the individual and intergroup level. In S. Oskamp (Ed.), *Reducing prejudice and discrimination*. Mahwah, NJ: Erlbaum.

Doyle, A. B., & Aboud, F. E. (1995). A longitudinal study of white children's racial prejudice as a social-cognitive development. *Merrill-Palmer Quarterly*, 41(2), 209–228.

Eisenberg, N., & Fabes, R. (1998). Prosocial development. In W. Damon (Ed.), *Handbook of child psychology*. New York: Wiley.

Fischer, A. R., & Shaw, C. M. (1999). African-American's mental health and perceptions of racist discrimination: The moderating effects of racial socialization experiences and self-esteem. *Journal of Counseling Psychology*, 46, 395–407.

Fisher, C. B., Jackson, J. F., Villarruel, F. A. (1998). The study of African-American and Latin-American children and youth. In W. Damon (Ed.), *Handbook of child psychology* (Vol. 1, 5th ed.), & R. Lerner (Vol. Ed.), *Theoretical models of human development*. New York: Wiley.

Fisher, C. B., Wallace, S. A., & Fenton, R. E. (2000). Discrimination distress during adolescence. *Journal of Youth and Adolescence*, 29, 679–695.

Gaertner, S. L., & Dovidio, J. F. (1986). The aversive form of racism. In J. F. Dovidio & S. L. Gaertner (Eds.), *Prejudice, discrimination, and racism*. Orlando, FL: Academic Press.

Gaertner, S. L., Rust, M. S., Dovidio, J. F., Bachman, B. A., & Anastasio, N. A. (1994). The contact hypothesis: The role of a common ingroup identity on reducing intergroup bias among majority and minority group members. *Small Group Research*, 25, 224–249.

Gary, L. E. (1995). African-American men's perceptions of racial discrimination: A sociocultural analysis. *Social Work Research*, 19, 207–216.

Gewirth, A. (1978). *Reason and morality*. Chicago: University of Chicago Press.

Gilligan, C. (1977). *In a different voice*. Cambridge: Harvard University Press.

Gould, S. J. (1981). *The mismeasure of man*. Cambridge: Harvard University Press.

Graham, S., & Juvonen, J. (1998). A social cognitive perspective on peer aggression and victimization. *Annals of Child Development*, 13, 21–66.

Graham, S., & Juvonen, J. (2001). An attributional approach to peer victimization. In J. Juvonen & S. Graham (Eds.), *Peer harassment in school: The plight of the vulnerable and victimized*. New York: Guilford Press.

Graham, S., & Taylor, A. (2002). Ethnicity, gender, and the development of achievement values. In A. Wigfield & J. Eccles (Eds.), *The development of achievement motivation*. San Diego: Academic Press.

Graves, J. L. (2001). *The emperor's new clothes: Biological theories of race at the millennium*. New Brunswick, NJ: Rutgers University Press.

Greenfield, P., & Cocking, R. (1994). *The cross-cultural roots of minority child development*. Mahwah, NJ: Erlbaum.

Grusec, J. E., & Goodnow, J. J. (1994). Impact of parental discipline methods on the child's internalization of values: A reconceptualization of current points of views. *Developmental Psychology*, **30**, 4–19.

Hamilton, D. L., & Sherman, J. W. (1994). Stereotypes. In R. S. Wyer, Jr., & T. K. Srull (Eds.), *Handbook of social cognition*, (2nd ed.). Hillsdale, NJ: Erlbaum.

Hawker, D. S. J., & Boulton, M. M. (2000). Twenty years' research on peer victimization and psychosocial maladjustment: A meta-analytic review of cross-sectional studies. *Journal of Child Psychology and Psychiatry & Allied Disciplines*, **41**, 441–455.

Helwig, C. C. (1995). Social context in social cognition: Psychological harm and civil liberties. In M. Killen & D. Hart (Eds.), *Morality in everyday life: Developmental perspectives*. Cambridge, England: Cambridge University Press.

Helwig, C. C. (1997). The role of agent and social context in judgments of freedom of speech and religion. *Child Development*, **68**, 484–495.

Helwig, C.C. (1998). Children's conceptions of fair government and freedom of speech. *Child Development*, **69**, 518–531.

Helwig, C. C., & Turiel, E. (2002). Children's social and moral reasoning. In C. Hart & P. Smith (Eds.), *Handbook of childhood social development*. Malden, MA: Blackwell.

Hirschfeld, L. A. (1995). Do children have a theory of race? *Cognition*, **54**, 209–252.

Horn, S. (in press). Adolescents' reasoning about exclusion from social groups. *Developmental Psychology*.

Horn, S., Killen, M., & Stangor, C. (1999). The influence of group stereotypes on adolescents' moral reasoning. *Journal of Early Adolescence*, **19**, 98–113.

Hymel, S., Bowker, A., & Woody, E. (1993). Aggressive versus withdrawn unpopular children: Variations in peer and self-perceptions in multiple domains. *Child Development*, **64**(3), 879–896.

Hymel, S., Wagner, E., & Butler, L. (1990). Reputational bias: View from the peer group. In S. R. Asher & J. Coie (Eds.), *Peer rejection in childhood*. Cambridge, England: Cambridge University Press.

Kahn, P. H. (1999). *The human relationship with nature*. Cambridge: MIT Press.

Katz, P. A., & Kofkin, J. A. (1997). Race, gender, and young children. In S. S. Luthar, J. A. Burack, D. Cicchetti, & J. Weisz (Eds.), *Developmental psychopathology: Perspectives on adjustment, risk, and disorder*. Cambridge, England: Cambridge University Press.

Katz, P. A., & Ksansnak, K. R. (1994). Developmental aspects of gender role flexibility and traditionality in middle childhood and adolescence. *Developmental Psychology*, **30**, 272–282.

Killen, M. (1991). Social and moral development in early childhood. In W. Kurtines & J. Gewirtz (Eds.), *Handbook of moral behavior and development* (Vol. 2). Hillsdale, NJ: Erlbaum.

Killen, M., Crystal, D., & Ruck, M. (2002). *The role of social experience on children's and adolescents' evaluation of exclusion and rights*. Unpublished manuscript, University of Maryland.

Killen, M., Crystal, D., & Watanabe, H. (2002). The individual and the group: Japanese and American children's evaluations of peer exclusion, tolerance of difference, and prescriptions for conformity. *Child Development*, **73**, 1788–1802.

Killen, M., & Hart, D. (Eds.). (1995). *Morality in everyday life: Developmental perspectives*. Cambridge, England: Cambridge University Press.

Killen, M., McGlothlin, H., & Lee-Kim, J. (2002). Between individuals and culture: Individuals' evaluations of exclusion from social groups. In H. Keller, Y. Poortinga, & A. Schoelmerich (Eds.), *Between biology and culture: Perspectives on ontogenetic development*. Cambridge, England: Cambridge University Press.

Killen, M., Pisacane, K., Lee-Kim, J., & Ardila-Rey, A. (2001). Fairness or stereotypes?: Young children's priorities when evaluating group inclusion and exclusion. *Developmental Psychology*, **37**(5), 587–596.

Killen, M., & Smetana, J.G. (1999). Social interactions in preschool classrooms and the development of young children's conceptions of the personal. *Child Development*, **70**, 486–501.

Killen, M., & Stangor, C. (2001). Children's social reasoning about inclusion and exclusion in gender and race peer group contexts. *Child Development*, **72**, 174–186.

Killen, M., Stangor, C., Price, B. S., Horn, S., & Sechrist, G. (2002). Racial exclusion in intimate relationships. Unpublished.

Killen, M., & Sueyoshi, L. (1995). Conflict resolution in Japanese social interactions. *Early Education and Development*, **6**, 313–330.

Killen, M., & Wainryb, C. (2000). Independence and interdependence in diverse cultural contexts. In S. Harkness and C. Raeff (Eds.), *Individualism and collectivism as cultural contexts for development*. Vol. 87 of *New Directions for Child Development*. San Francisco: Jossey-Bass.

Knight, G. P., Bernal, M. E., Cota, M. K., Garza, C. A., & Ocampo, K. A. (1993). Family socialization and Mexican-American identity and behavior. In M. E. Bernal & G. P. Knight (Eds.), *Ethnic identity: Formation and transmission among Hispanics and other minorities*. Albany: State University of New York Press.

Koblinsky, S. G., Cruse, D. F., & Sagawara, A. I. (1978). Sex role stereotypes and children's memory for story content. *Child Development*, **49**, 452–458.

Kochenderfer-Ladd, B., & Ladd, G. (2001). Variations in peer victimization: Relations to children's maladjustment. In J. Juvonen & S. Graham (Eds.), *Peer harassment in school: The plight of the vulnerable and victimized*. New York: Guilford Press.

Kohlberg, L. (1969). Stage and sequence: The cognitive-developmental approach to socialization. In D. Goslin (Ed.), *Handbook of socialization theory and research*. Chicago: Rand McNally.

Kohlberg, L. (1971). From is to ought: How to commit the naturalistic fallacy and get away with it in the study of moral development. In T. Mischel (Ed.), *Psychology and genetic epistemology*. New York: Academic Press.

Kohlberg, L. (1984). *Essays on moral development: The psychology of moral development*. San Francisco: Harper and Row.

Kuhn, D., Nash, S. C., & Brucken, L. (1978). Sex role concepts of two- and three-year olds. *Child Development*, **49**, 445–451.

Laupa, M. (1986). Children's reasoning about authority in home and school contexts. *Social Development*, **4**(1), 1–16.

Laursen, B., & Williams, V. A. (1997). Perceptions of interdependence and closeness among adolescents with and without romantic partners. In S. Shulman & W. A. Collins (Eds.), *Romantic relationships in adolescence: Developmental perspectives. Vol 78: New Directions for Child Development*. San Francisco: Jossey-Bass.

Leary, M. (1990). Responses to social exclusion: Social anxiety, jealousy, loneliness, depression, and low self-esteem. *Journal of Social and Clinical Psychology*, **9**, 221–229.

Leyens, J. P., Yzerbyt, V. Y., & Schadron, G. H. (1994). *Stereotypes and social cognition*. London: Sage.

Lee-Kim, J. (2002). Korean children's and parents' conceptions of gender-role expectations in the family and cultural contexts. Unpublished manuscript, University of Maryland.

Liben, L. S., & Signorella, M. L. (1993). Gender-schematic processing in children: The role of initial interpretations of stimuli. *Developmental Psychology*, **29**, 141–149.

Loury, G. C. (2002). *The anatomy of racial inequality*. Cambridge: Harvard University Press.

Maccoby, E. (2000). Perspectives on gender development. *International Journal of Behavioral Development*, **24**(4), 398–406.

Mackie, D. M., Hamilton, D. L., Susskind, J., & Rosselli, F. (1996). Social psychological foundations of stereotype formation. In C. Macrae, C. Stangor, & M. Hewstone (Eds.), *Stereotypes and stereotyping*. New York: Guilford Press.

Macrae, C. N., Stangor, C., & Hewstone, M. (Eds.). (1996). *Stereotypes and stereotyping*. New York: Guilford Press.

Martin, C. L. (1989). Children's use of gender-related information in making social judgments. *Developmental Psychology*, **25**(1), 80–88.

Martin, C. L., & Halverson, C. F. (1981). A schematic processing model of sex-typing and stereotyping in children. *Child Development*, **52**, 119–1134.

Martin, C. L., Wood, C. H., & Little, J. K. (1990). The development of gender stereotype components. *Child Development*, **61**, 1891–1904.

McGlothlin, H., Killen, M., & Edmonds, C. (2002). *Implicit racial biases in children's judgments about friendship and social relationships*. Unpublished manuscript, University of Maryland.

McLoyd, V. C., & Randolph, S. M. (1986). Secular trends in the study of Afro-American children: A review of child development, 1936–1980. *Monographs of the Society for Research in Child Development*, **50** (4, Serial No. 5).

Miller, J., & Luthar, S. (1989). Issues of interpersonal responsibility and accountability: A comparison of Indians' and Americans' moral judgments. *Social Cognition*, **7**(3), 237–261.

Minow, M. (1990). *Making all the difference: Inclusion, exclusion, and American law*. Ithaca, NY: Cornell University Press.

Moffitt, T. (1993). Adolescence-limited and life-course-persistent antisocial behavior: A developmental taxonomy. *Psychological Review*, **100**, 674–701.

Nagel, T. (1979). *Mortal questions*. Cambridge, England: Cambridge University Press.

National Research Council and Institute of Medicine (2000). *Improving intergroup relations among youth: Summary of a research workshop. Forum on adolescence, board on children, youth and families, Commission on behavioral and social sciences and education*. Washington, DC: National Academy Press.

Newcombe, A. F., & Bukowski, W. M. (1984). A longitudinal study of the utility of social preference and social impact sociometric classification schemes. *Child Development*, **55**, 1434–1447.

Nucci, L. P. (1981). Conceptions of personal issues: A domain distinct from moral or societal concepts. *Child Development*, **52**(1), 114–121.

Nucci, L. P. (1996). Morality and the personal sphere of actions. In E. S. Reed, E. Turiel, & T. Brown (Eds.), *Values and knowledge*. Mahwah, NJ: Erlbaum.

Nucci, L. P. (2001). *Education in the moral domain*. Cambridge, England: Cambridge University Press.

Nucci, L. P., Camino, C., & Milnitsky-Sapiro, C. (1996). Social class effects on Northeastern Brazilian children's conceptions of areas of personal choice and social regulation. *Child Development*, **67**, 1223–1242.

Nucci, L. P., Guerra, N., & Lee, J. (1991). Adolescent judgments of the personal, prudential, and normative aspects of drug usage. *Developmental Psychology*, **27**, 841–848.

Nucci, L. P., & Herman, S. (1982). Behavioral disordered children's conceptions of moral, conventional, and personal issues. *Journal of Abnormal Child Psychology*, **10**, 411–426.

Nucci, L. P., Killen, M., & Smetana, J. G. (1996). Autonomy and the personal: Negotiation and social reciprocity in adult-child social exchanges. In M. Killen (Ed.), *Children's autonomy, social competence, and interactions with adults and other children: Exploring connections and consequences. Vol. 73: New Directions for Child Development*. San Francisco: Jossey-Bass

Nucci, L. P., & Lee, J. Y. (1993). Morality and autonomy. In G. G. Noam & T. E. Wren (Eds.), *The moral self.* Cambridge: MIT Press.

Nucci, L. P., & Turiel, E. (1978). Social interactions and the development of social concepts in preschool children. *Child Development,* **49**, 400–407.

Nucci, L. P., & Turiel, E. (1993). God's word, religious rules, and their relation to Christian and Jewish children's concepts of morality. *Child Development,* **64**(5), 1475–1491.

Nussbaum, M. (1999). *Sex and social justice.* Oxford, England: Oxford University Press.

Ogbu, J. (1991). Immigrant and involuntary minorities in comparative perspective. In M. G. Gibson & J. U. Ogbu (Eds.), *Minority status and schooling.* New York: Garland.

Ogbu, J. (1994). From cultural differences to differences in cultural frame of reference. In P. Greenfield & R. Cocking (Eds.), *Cross-cultural roots of minority child development* (pp. 365–391). Mahwah, NJ: Erlbaum.

Okin, S. M. (1989). *Justice, gender, and the family.* New York: Basic Books.

Okin, S. M. (1999). *Is multiculturalism bad for women?* Princeton, NJ: Princeton University Press.

Olweus, D. (1993). Victimization by peers: Antecedents and long-term outcomes. In K. H. Rubin & J. B. Asendorf (Eds.), *Social withdrawal, inhibition, and shyness in childhood.* Mahwah, NJ: Erlbaum.

Opotow, S. (1990). Moral exclusion and injustice: An introduction. *Journal of Social Issues,* **46**, 1–20.

Oskamp, S. (Ed.). (2000). *Reducing prejudice and discrimination.* Mahwah, NJ: Erlbaum.

Park, B., Ryan, C. S., & Judd, C. M. (1992). Role of meaningful subgroups in explaining differences in perceived variability for in-groups and out-groups. *Journal of Personality and Social Psychology,* **63**, 553–567.

Parkhurst, J., & Asher, S. (1992). Peer rejection in middle school: Subgroup differences in behavior, loneliness, and interpersonal concerns. *Developmental Psychology,* **28**(2), 231–241.

Pessar, P. R. (1999). The role of gender, households, and social networks in the migration process: A review. In C. Hirschman, P. Kasinitz, & J. DeWind (Eds.), *The handbook of international migration: The American experience.* New York: Russell Sage Foundation.

Pettigrew, T. (1998). Intergroup contact theory. *American Review of Psychology,* **49**, 65–85.

Pettigrew, T., & Tropp, L. (2000). Does intergroup contact reduce prejudice?: Recent meta-analytic findings. In S. Oskamp (Ed.), *Reducing prejudice and discrimination.* Mahwah, NJ: Erlbaum.

Phinney, J. (1990). Ethnic identity in adolescents and adults: Review of research. *Psychological Bulletin,* **108**, 499–514.

Phinney, J., Cantu, C., & Kurtz, D. (1997). Ethnic and American identity as predictors of self-esteem among African-American, Latino, and White adolescents. *Journal of Youth and Adolescence,* **26**, 165–185.

Piaget, J. (1932). *The moral judgment of the child.* New York: Free Press.

Powlishta, K. K. (1995). Gender bias in children's perceptions of personality traits. *Sex Roles,* **32**, 17–28.

Prencipe, A., & Helwig, C. (2002). The development of reasoning about the teaching of values in school and family contexts. *Child Development,* **73**, 841–856.

Putallaz, M., & Wasserman, A. (1990). Children's entry behavior. In S. R. Asher & J. D. Coie (Eds.), *Peer rejection in childhood.* Cambridge, England: Cambridge University Press.

Roemer, J. E. (1998). *Equality of opportunity.* Cambridge: Harvard University Press.

Rolandelli, D. R. (1991). Gender role portrayal analysis of children's television programming in Japan. *Human Relations,* **44**, 1273–1299.

Rubin, K. H., Bukowski, W., & Parker, J. (1998). Peer interactions, relationships and groups. In W. Damon (Series Ed.), *Handbook of child psychology,* & N. Eisenberg (Vol. Ed.), *Vol 3. Socialization.* New York: Wiley.

Rubin, K. H., Coplan, R. J., Nelson, L. J., Cheah, C. S., & Lagace-Seguin, D. G. (1999). Peer relationships in childhood. In M. H. Bornstein & M. E. Lamb (Eds.), *Developmental psychology: An advanced textbook* (4th ed.). Mahwah, NJ: Erlbaum.

Rubin, K. H., & Krasnor, L. R. (1986). Social-cognitive and social behavioral perspectives on problem solving. In M. Perlmutter (Ed.), *Cognitive perspective on children's social and behavioral development. The Minnesota Symposia on Child Psychology* (Vol. 18). Hillsdale, NJ: Erlbaum.

Ruble, D., & Martin, C. (1998). Gender development. In W. Damon (Ed.), *Handbook of child psychology* N. Eisenberg, (Vol. Ed.). *Vol. 3. Socialization.* New York: Wiley.

Ruck, M. D., Abramovitch, R., & Keating, D. (1998). Children's and adolescents' understanding of rights: Balancing nurturance and self-determination. *Child Development,* **64**, 404–417.

Ruck, M. D., & Wortley, S. (2002). Racial and ethnic minority high school students' perceptions of school disciplinary practices: A look at some Canadian findings. *Journal of Youth and Adolescence,* **31**, 185–195.

Rumbaut, R. G., & Portes, A. (Eds.). (2001). *Ethnicities: Children of immigrants in America.* New York: Russell Sage Foundation.

Sagar, H. A., & Schofield, J. W. (1980). Racial and behavioral cues in Black and White children's perceptions of ambiguously aggressive acts. *Journal of Personality and Social Psychology,* **39**, 590–598.

Sears, D. O., & Levy, S. (in press). Child and adult development. In D. O. Sears, L. Huddy, & R. L. Jervis (Eds.), *Handbook of political psychology.* Oxford, England: Oxford University Press.

Sherif, M. (1966). *Group conflict and cooperation.* London: Routledge & Kegan Paul.

Shulman, S., & Scharf, M. (2000). Adolescent romantic behaviors and perceptions: Age- and gender-related differences, and links with family and peer relationships. *Journal of Research on Adolescence,* **10**, 99–118.

Skrentny, J. D. (1996). *The ironies of affirmative action: Politics, culture, and justice in America.* Chicago: University of Chicago Press.

Smetana, J. G. (1984). Toddlers' social interactions regarding moral and conventional transgressions. *Child Development,* **55**, 1767–1776.

Smetana, J. G. (1988). Adolescents' and parents' conceptions of parental authority. *Child Development,* **59**(2), 321–335.

Smetana, J. G. (1989a). Adolescents' and parents' reasoning about actual family conflict. *Child Development,* **60**(5), 1052–1067.

Smetana, J. G. (1989b). Toddlers' social interactions in the context of moral and conventional transgressions in the home. *Developmental Psychology,* **25**(4), 499–508.

Smetana, J. G. (1995). Morality in context: Abstractions, ambiguities, and applications. In R. Vasta (Ed.), *Annals of child development* (Vol. 10). London: Jessica Kinglsey.

Smetana, J. G. (1997). Parenting and the development of social knowledge reconceptualized: A social domain analysis. In J. E. Grusec & L. Kuczynski (Eds.), *Parenting and children's internalization of values.* New York: Wiley

Smetana, J. G., & Bitz, B. (1996). Adolescents' conceptions of teachers' authority and their relations to rule violations in school. *Child Development,* **67**(3), 1153–1172.

Smetana, J. G., & Braeges, J. (1990). The development of toddler's moral and conventional judgments. *Merrill-Palmer Quarterly,* **36**(3), 329–346.

Smetana, J. G., & Gaines, C. (1999). Adolescent-parent conflict in middle-class African American families. *Child Development,* **70**(6), 1447–1463.

Smetana, J. G., Killen, M., & Turiel, E. (1991). Children's reasoning about interpersonal and moral conflicts. *Child Development,* **62**, 629–644.

Stangor, C., & McMillan, D. (1992). Memory for expectancy-congruent and expectancy-incongruent information: A review of the social and social developmental literatures. *Psychological Bulletin*, 111(1), 42–61.

Stangor, C., & Ruble, D. N. (1989). Differential influences of gender schematic and gender constancy on children's information processing behavior. *Social Cognition*, 7, 353–372.

Stangor, C., & Schaller, M. (1996). Stereotypes as individual and collective representations. In C. N. Macrae, C. Stangor, & M. Hewstone (Eds.), *Stereotypes and stereotyping*. New York: Guilford Press.

Staub, E. (1987). *The roots of evil: The origins of genocide and other group violence*. Cambridge, England: Cambridge University Press.

Staub, E. (1990). Moral exclusion, personal goal theory, and extreme destructiveness. *Journal of Social Issues*, 46(1), 47–64.

Steele, C. (1997). A threat in the air. How stereotypes shape intellectual identity and performance. *American Psychologist*, 52, 613–629.

Steele, C. & Aronson, J. (1995). Stereotype threat and the intellectual test performance of African Americans. *Journal of Personality & Social Psychology*, 69, 797–811.

Stoddart, T., & Turiel, E. (1985). Children's concepts of cross-gender activities. *Child Development*, 56, 1241–1252

Tajfel, H., Billig, M., Bundy, R. P., & Flament, C. (1971). Social categorization and intergroup behavior. *European Journal of Social Psychology*, 1, 149–177.

Tajfel, H., & Turner, J. C. (1979). An integrative theory of intergroup conflict. In W. G. Austin & S. Worchel (Eds.), *The social psychology of intergroup relations*. Monterey, CA: Brooks/Cole.

Theimer, C. E., Killen, M., & Stangor, C. (2001). Preschool children's evaluations of exclusion in gender-stereotypic contexts. *Developmental Psychology*, 37, 1–10.

Tisak, M. (1995). Domains of social reasoning and beyond. In R. Vasta (Ed.), *Annals of child development* (Vol. 11). London: Jessica Kingsley Publishers.

Tisak, M., & Turiel, E. (1984). Children's conceptions of moral and prudential rules. *Child Development*, 55, 1030–1039.

Turiel, E. (1983). *The development of social knowledge: Morality and convention*. Cambridge, England: Cambridge University Press.

Turiel, E. (1998). The development of morality. In W. Damon (Series Ed.), *Handbook of child psychology*, & N. Eisenberg (Vol. Ed.), *Vol. 3, Socialization*. New York: Wiley.

Turiel, E. (2002). *The culture of morality*. Cambridge, England: Cambridge University Press.

Turiel, E., Hildebrandt, C., & Wainryb, C. (1985). Judging social issues: Difficulties, inconsistencies, and consistencies. *Monographs of the Society for Research in Child Development*, 56 (2, Serial No. 224).

Turiel, E., Killen, M., & Helwig, C. C. (1987). Morality: Its structure, functions, and vagaries. In J. Kagan & S. Lamb (Eds.), *The emergence of morality in young children*. Chicago: University of Chicago Press.

Turiel, E., & Wainryb, C. (1998). Concepts of freedoms and rights in a traditional, hierarchically organized society. *British Journal of Developmental Psychology*, 16(3), 375–395.

Wainryb, C. (1991). Understanding differences in moral judgments: The role of informational assumptions. *Child Development*, 62, 840–851.

Wainryb, C., Shaw, L. A., & Maianu, C. (1998). Tolerance and intolerance: Children's and adolescents' judgments of dissenting beliefs, speech, persons, and conduct. *Child Development*, 69(6), 1541–1555.

Wainryb, C., & Turiel, E. (1994). Dominance, subordination, and concepts of personal entitlements in cultural contexts. *Child Development*, 65, 1701–1722.

Welch-Ross, M. K., & Schmidt, C. R. (1996). Gender-schema development and children's constructive story memory: Evidence for a developmental model. *Child Development*, 67, 820–835.

Wentzel, K. R., & Erdley, C. A. (1993). Strategies for making friends: Relations to social behavior and peer acceptance in early adolescence. *Developmental Psychology, 29*(5), 819–826.

Winer, G. A., & McGlone, C. (1993). On the uncertainty of conservation: Responses to misleading conservation questions. *Developmental Psychology, 29*, 760–769.

Yee, M. D., & Brown, R. J. (1992). Self evaluations and intergroup attitudes in children aged three to nine. *Child Development, 63*, 619–629.

Youniss, J., McLellan, J. A., & Strouse, D. (1994). We're popular, but we're not snobs: Adolescents describe their crowds. In R. Montemayor, G. R. Adams, & T. P. Gullotta (Eds.), *Personal relationships during adolescence.* Thousand Oaks, CA: Sage.

Youniss, J., & Smollar, J. (1985). *Adolescent relations with mothers, fathers, and friends.* Chicago: University of Chicago Press.

ACKNOWLEDGMENTS

This project was supported by grants from the National Science Foundation (BCS9729739) and the National Institute of Child Health and Human Development (HD41421-01), and two awards from the University of Maryland Graduate Research Board. Part of this project was presented as a paper at the Biennial Meeting of the Society for Research in Child Development, Minneapolis, MN, April 2001, and the Annual Symposium of the Jean Piaget Society, June 2002.

We thank the following students for their assistance with data collection, Alicia Ardila-Rey, Holly Bozeman, Christina Edmonds, Rachel Garcia, Nicole Gresham, Avital Herbin, Keidra Lazard, Nancy Margie, Susie Park, Aaron Schneider, Megan Scott, Nicole Searfoss, Gretchen Sechrist, Stefanie Sinno, Jacilyn Smith, Avy Stock, Alexis Williams, Solmaz Zabiheian, and Katherine Zukowski, and with data analyses, Nancy Margie and Stefanie Sinno.

We extend our appreciation to the Montgomery County Public Schools in Maryland, U.S.A., for their willingness to allow this study to be conducted in their school system, as well as to the principals and teachers who participated. We thank Joseph Hawkins for encouraging us to pursue this avenue of research. We greatly appreciate the insightful feedback and thorough comments from the Editor, Willis Overton, and from three anonymous reviewers. In addition, we thank Judi Smetana for her helpful suggestions on the manuscript. We are grateful to the parents who gave their consent, and to the students for their willingness to participate in this project.

Correspondence concerning this article should be addressed to Melanie Killen, Department of Human Development, 3304 Benjamin Building, University of Maryland, 20742-1131 (mkillen@umd.edu), office phone: 301.405.3176.

COMMENTARY

IS IT EVER OK TO EXCLUDE ON THE BASIS OF RACE OR GENDER?: THE ROLE OF CONTEXT, STEREOTYPES, AND HISTORICAL CHANGE

Charles C. Helwig

Exclusion takes many forms in contemporary society, sometimes with harmful outcomes. For example, differential access to economic resources and high-quality education or healthcare may have moral implications for social equality and individual welfare. However, many previously accepted systems of exclusion sanctioned by law, such as those based on race or gender, have been largely dismantled in Western societies over the past century (e.g., school desegregation in the United States and Apartheid in South Africa). Even so, problems arising from intentional or unintentional acts of racial or gender exclusion continue to plague many societies, including modern democracies. Examples from the current American social and political context include the persistence of gender inequalities in wages despite legislation designed specifically to address sex discrimination, the disproportionate representation of African Americans among the nation's poor, and, more recently, concerns about racial profiling of Arab Americans and the secret detention of immigrants from Muslim countries following the terrorist attacks of September 11, 2001. The more we know about how individuals understand and think about a variety of forms of exclusion, the better we may be able to address its harmful manifestations in society.

In this *Monograph*, Melanie Killen, Jennie Lee-Kim, Heidi McGlothlin, and Charles Stangor report the results of a large-scale investigation of children's and adolescents' reasoning about racial and gender exclusion in the context of friendship relations, the peer group, and the school. They offer a whole new way of looking at the phenomenon of exclusion that vastly expands our range of vision and promises to revolutionize work in this area. To fully appreciate what they have accomplished, it is

120

necessary first to briefly review some of the major existing perspectives through which exclusion has been examined in developmental and social psychological research, and to consider some of the limitations of past approaches.

Previous Perspectives on Exclusion

One perspective on exclusion, encompassing social psychological research by Opotow (1990) and Staub (1987) and extending to current developmental work on "relational aggression" (Crick & Grotpeter, 1995), focuses attention on the antisocial motives of those who exclude. As an example, Killen and colleagues cite the following definition of moral exclusion given by Opotow: "when individuals or groups are perceived as outside the boundaries in which moral values, rules, and considerations of fairness apply" (p. 1). Exclusion, in this approach, is defined as strictly moral in nature. The notion of moral exclusion is certainly useful in accounting for extreme cases of immorality and injustice, including practices such as slavery and genocide. This leaves open the question of to what extent it can account for other kinds of exclusion—even those based on gender or race—found in modern, democratic societies in which the moral equality of persons may be assumed.

As Killen and colleagues suggest, and as their data bear out, not all forms of exclusion result from simply defining others as beyond the bounds of morality. For example, concerns over such issues as the smooth functioning of voluntary social groups or the right of individuals to select their friends using criteria of their own choosing may be reasons for some forms of exclusion. To apply a model such as Opotow's in a comprehensive way to account for all forms of exclusion in contemporary society runs the risk of the "demonization" of a large segment of the population, and presents difficulties in accounting for the heterogeneity evident in people's judgments and reasoning about exclusion.

A second perspective, encountered in developmental psychological research on peer relations, has focused on how exclusion is related to various characteristics of the recipient or victim of exclusion, such as aggressiveness or social withdrawal (Hymel, Wagner, & Butler, 1990). This individual deficit model has shown that exclusion may, at times, be accounted for by reciprocal processes, in which the behavior of the excluded interacts with and may contribute to the exclusionary attitudes and behaviors of others. But the individual social deficit model has not been applied to exclusion motivated by categorical judgments about individuals based on group attributes such as race or gender. This is understandable because, in these cases, applying this model would be inappropriate and could lead to charges of "blaming the victim." Certainly discrimination and prejudice may produce behavioral manifestations in its victims similar to those seen in other instances of peer rejection (e.g., social withdrawal), but more fundamental to understanding this kind of exclusion are the prior attitudes and beliefs about gender or race that are its true precipitating causes.

A third perspective has been to investigate exclusion from the standpoint of cognitive processes. Social psychologists, in particular, have documented ways in which stereotypes, attitude structures, and selective information processing strategies may lead to prejudicial or discriminatory outcomes (Mackie, Hamilton, Susskind, & Rosselli, 1996). Although cognition figures importantly in this work, the types of cognitive processes proposed by social psychologists stay relatively close to the surface, and a deeper analysis of moral reasoning is often neglected. Instead, social psychologists have typically preferred explanations of exclusion that rely on general mechanisms such as in-group favoritism and the desire to protect one's own group from perceived threats by others (Fiske, 2002).

In contrast, developmental psychologists have studied moral reasoning, but prior to the social domain perspective guiding the work described in this *Monograph*, their research was carried out mainly in the context of global stage theories such as those of Kohlberg or Piaget. In global stage approaches, moral reasoning is presumed to follow general developmental patterns, in which egoistic perspectives are supplanted in development by perspectives focusing on social groups and norms, which in turn are supplanted (in late adolescence or adulthood) by perspectives favoring equality, due process, and universal human rights (Kohlberg, 1984). Researchers who have adopted a general stage approach have tended to study moral reasoning using a predetermined set of hypothetical dilemmas covering a range of different social and moral concepts, but they have not specifically looked at reasoning about exclusion in everyday social contexts.

A New Approach: Social Domains and the Role of Context

Killen and colleagues' approach sits squarely within the cognitive perspective in its emphasis on how individuals construe, interpret, and reason about exclusion. Their approach makes room for stereotypes, or general attitudes held by individuals about social groups, as well as the deeper conceptual categories and forms of reasoning that individuals bring to bear in making judgments about exclusion. Exclusion is conceptualized as a multidimensional construct that is influenced by the diverse social judgments made by individuals in different kinds of social situations. Their major point—that not all forms of exclusion may be conceptualized as moral—is clearly and convincingly brought out in their data. Their research findings indicate that when children and adolescents reason about exclusion in friendship contexts, they often rely on concepts of personal choice or jurisdiction in support of individuals' freedom to choose their close friends. When they reason about exclusion in social groups such as clubs, they often rely on social organizational concepts such as group functioning and shared social norms. And, when they reason about exclusion in school contexts, they overwhelmingly apply moral concepts pertaining to human rights, justice, and the harmful effects of exclusion on individuals or society. These three forms of reasoning parallel findings from the large body of research on social domains (Turiel, 1998; Smetana, 1995), which shows that individuals distinguish personal, social conventional, and moral domains in their reasoning and that they apply these different forms of thinking to different kinds of situations.

This theoretical approach can explain several facets of the research findings better than the other approaches. One of the major findings is that reasoning and judgments about exclusion vary by context. Individuals do indeed consider the moral aspects of exclusion, but the same study participants who in some situations rejected exclusionary practices based on moral reasoning would in other situations subordinate morality to concerns such as personal choice or group functioning. As Killen and her colleagues point out, only "a small minority of participants . . . condoned exclusion across a range of contexts and used much less moral reasoning than most of the participants in the study." Perhaps constructs such as Opotow's moral exclusion model may be able to explain the responses of this small proportion of participants, but the judgments of most individuals varied by social context in ways that seem better accounted for by the social domain model.

More generally, these findings raise questions about attempts to account for exclusion solely in terms of broad personological variables, such as prejudice. To be sure, variation was found to exist within contexts in people's tendency to focus on either moral or nonmoral features in their judgments, but even those who thought it was acceptable to exclude in some contexts also took issues of rights and justice seriously and applied these concepts in other situations to denounce exclusion. No clear typology of persons—for example, as excluders versus nonexcluders—emerges from these data. The results illustrate how seeming inconsistencies in judgments can be made sense of by exploring the reasoning that motivates the different types of judgments people may make in different situations. In short, context appears to be at least as important as individual dispositional properties in explaining judgments of exclusion.

Nor did general stages of reasoning seem to be of much use here. As noted, reasoning within individuals spanned a broad array of concerns, including a focus on the desires and interests of the self (personal choice), the social organizational conventions and norms of the group, and universal principles of justice and human rights, in ways that were accounted for more by context than by age-sequential stages of moral reasoning. In fact, one of the more surprising findings was that individuals sometimes become *more* accepting of exclusion with age, rather than less. This runs counter to straightforward cognitive-developmental theories (Kohlberg, 1984) wherein it is maintained that social reasoning progresses with age toward more advanced forms in which the focus is on principles of universal human rights and equality. Rather, as individuals develop more complex understandings of social organizations and groups, they seem to be more willing to subordinate the equal treatment of others to group goals, but only in some contexts and not others.

And finally, although Killen and colleagues found evidence that stereotypes were used to support exclusion in some instances, they found few traces of some of the usual phenomena social psychologists have proposed to account for exclusion, such as in-group bias. For example, when the target of the exclusion was Blacks, the White participants were on the whole no more likely to condone exclusion than were the Black participants. I think these findings provide powerful support for the need to approach judgments of exclusion from the perspective of reasoning processes, rather than through the more simplistic and mechanistic explanations, such as in-group/out-group bias, that are common to contemporary social psychological models. Reasoning does matter, but this only becomes fully apparent when our models of social thought are sufficiently differentiated to account for the diverse kinds of reasoning people use in different social contexts.

The Role of Stereotypes

Having considered some of the merits of this study, let us look at some further avenues for research. Deeper exploration is needed of the role played by assumptions about the features of persons, including stereotypes, that may underlie and help explain some of the contextual variations found in judgments and reasoning. Assumptions about race- or gender-based individual and group characteristics, including stereotypes, emerged in their data in some instances but not others, and were sometimes used to justify exclusion. For example, assumptions sometimes were made about differences in interests or differences in personality characteristics associated with gender or race that were believed to have an impact on the smooth functioning of friendships or social groups. These differences were seen as irrelevant to the school context, however, as participants frequently referred to universal features of persons (e.g., "everyone has the same brain") in support of the proposition that education is a universal human right. This is an illustration of how the perceived goals and purposes of friendship, peer, and school contexts vary, and how questions of exclusion may engage assumptions about the different features of personhood that may factor into individuals' judgments and reasoning in different contexts. In other words, stereotypes matter too, but they need to be understood in conjunction with social context in order to get a full picture of the complexity of individuals' reasoning.

Of course, assumptions held about persons, including stereotypes, vary across individuals, and indeed some participants focused on the similarities between genders or races while others focused on the differences. The assumptions people hold about others, and how these assumptions may help to account for diverse judgments about exclusion, are important avenues for future research. In particular, we need a clearer picture of why some individuals rely on stereotypes in some instances while others do not. The "folk theories" that people may hold about the origins of perceived gender and racial differences could be relevant here.

Some intriguing findings from a recent study begin to shed light on some of these issues. Neff and Terry-Schmitt (2002) examined whether attitudes toward gender equality among adolescents and young adults are related to whether they believe that the sources of sex-role traits are to be found in biological, social, or religious (divine) causes. They found that the belief that the causes of gender differences are social in nature (e.g., related to differences in socialization or opportunities) was significantly related to egalitarian attitudes about gender. In contrast, belief in the religious or divine origins of gender differences (e.g., that they reflect God's plan for how men and women should be) was related to traditional (hierarchical) attitudes about gender. Interestingly, a sex difference emerged in the role played by biological attributions (e.g., genes, hormones, brain structure). Biological attributions were related to traditional or hierarchical attitudes, but only for males; there was no such association for females. This finding suggests that although many females may hold biological assumptions about sex differences, they are less likely than males to see these biological differences as sufficient to justify gender inequality. Perhaps this may help account for Killen and colleagues' finding that males in some cases are more willing than females to accept exclusionary practices regarding women in other cultures. More generally, I think that an in-depth examination of the implicit theories people hold about the sources of gender and racial differences may help us to understand the operation of judgments of exclusion as applied in different social contexts, including that of culture.

The Role of Historical Change

Throughout history, there have been changing assumptions about the features believed to be shared by individuals from different social groups, including their personalities, capacities, and abilities. In the past, these assumptions were sometimes appealed to as a basis for denying or affirming basic rights of different kinds to different classes of agents. For example, slavery was justified by appeal to the presumed natural and moral inferiority of a class of persons (Blacks). Similarly, the right to vote was denied to women long after men enjoyed it, a distinction based on assumptions about women's natural dependency and inferiority. Even figures of the American Revolution, such as John Adams, argued that voting rights should be restricted to men who held property, showing how even a "democrat" who holds sophisticated conceptions of democracy in one context may, at the same time, apply these concepts in ways that seem, to our sensibilities, astonishingly narrow (Rosi, 1973).

In the present study, Killen and colleagues have classified exclusion in the schools based on race or gender as a moral event, and the responses of their American research participants clearly have borne out this classification. But American schools were permitted to exclude on the basis of race until the historic Supreme Court decision in 1954 mandating desegregation of the public schools. Clearly, judgments about the morality of exclusion in a variety of contexts have changed throughout history, presumably in parallel with changes in assumptions about racial or gender differences in morally relevant human characteristics and capacities. Yet, as this study (and that of Neff & Terry-Schmitt, 2002) demonstrates, assumptions about attributes believed to be associated with race or gender do persist for many individuals today and are used by them to justify some forms of exclusion and inequality. It should be emphasized, however, that both the particular assumptions about differences held, and the forms of exclusion that these assumptions may be believed to permit, certainly have become much more benign than in the past. One question is whether, with time, the contextual differences that Killen and her colleagues have uncovered will also disappear, as have these other distinctions. If this study were to be replicated 50 or 100 years from now, what would we find?

If I may be so reckless as to hazard a prediction, I would expect that, using the measures of this *Monograph*, many of the contextual differences will have indeed diminished. As barriers break down between genders and races, and people in general become both more similar in some respects and more respectful of their remaining differences, I expect that the notion of race or gender as a legitimate basis for friendship choices or group memberships will seem as alien (and perhaps as immoral) as exclusion in the school example. This is not to suggest that because the findings might vary over time the differences between the social contexts studied in this *Monograph* are not enduring and important. Instead, I think that the assessment questions used in this study actually underestimate the potential differences between contexts that could have been found and that will continue to be seen well into the future.

Killen and colleagues asked their participants whether it is all right for individuals to exclude. I might imagine that at least two different kinds of underlying judgments could have contributed to participants' responses to this question, in varying (but unknown) degrees: (a) how good or bad it is for individuals to make such decisions, and (b) whether individuals are perceived as having a right to make such decisions. The first pertains to evaluative judgments about the particular act in question (i.e., exclusion); the second pertains to whether or not individuals may be legitimately prohibited from exercising their choices (e.g., by laws or restrictive regulations). I believe that the former judgment is especially likely to be influenced by prevailing social attitudes governing race and gender, and thus may be expected to vary greatly over time. For example, 100 or more years ago, a majority of people might have thought it perfectly fine for individuals to choose their friends on the basis of race and gender, and I suspect that they may even have looked at cross-race or cross-gender friendships as being rather odd. Today, however, it appears that most people (78% in Killen et al.'s American sample) think it is wrong to discriminate in this way. However, from a rights perspective, it could still be acknowledged that in some cases, people have the right to do things that we consider morally objectionable. For example, I do not think that governments should pass laws prohibiting individuals from choosing their friendships on such a basis or that governments should punish them in any way, even though I deplore this practice. In contrast, I would judge that a public school that discriminated on the basis of race or gender should be shut down.

Some data from a study I conducted with a colleague (Prencipe & Helwig, 2002) suggest that individuals in North America do distinguish between judgments of legal regulation and evaluations of acts in just these sorts of ways. We found that Canadian children and young adults overwhelmingly believe it is not permissible for parents to teach their children various antisocial values, such as prejudice, laziness, or antidemocratic beliefs, and yet most older adolescents and adults believe that it would be wrong for the government to outlaw the teaching of these values within the family. (They do think that their teaching should be outlawed in the school, however.) To fully capture the nature of the differences between contexts such as those of friendship, the peer group, and the school, I believe it will be useful to employ more differentiated assessment mea-

127

sures. In addition to investigating judgments of acts of exclusion, future research might look at issues such as individuals' judgments of the motivations of those who exclude, and, most important, their understanding of the legitimate boundaries of legal regulation in different contexts (public and private). I believe that the notion apparently appealed to by many participants in this study of a personal sphere immune from governmental regulation will endure in American society, despite significant changes that will continue to occur in social attitudes about exclusionary personal choices.

Conclusion

This is a landmark study that simultaneously opens up a whole new line of investigation and helps us to make sense of prior research findings. The approach of Killen, Lee-Kim, McGlothlin, and Stangor has admirable breadth in its ability to embrace and explain variations in judgments and reasoning across social contexts and to incorporate the insights and findings of other perspectives, such as social psychological research on stereotypes, without reducing social thinking to simplistic or mechanistic, catch-all processes. Along with this breadth, their approach is also rigorous in drawing on explanations of social and moral reasoning that emphasize well-defined and extensively investigated domains of social thought. They have shown us that both reasoning and context are important and must be considered together to understand certain forms of social exclusion. I have no doubt that they—and those who follow in their footsteps—will continue to refine this approach as more is understood about the roles played by folk theories about groups (including stereotypes) and conceptions of public and private spheres in accounting for individuals' attitudes, judgments, and social reasoning regarding exclusion.

Acknowledgments

The author's work on this commentary was partly supported by a grant from the Social Sciences and Humanities Research Council of Canada.

References

Crick, N., & Grotpeter, J. (1995). Relational aggression, gender, and social psychological adjustment. *Child Development, 66,* 710–722.

Fiske, S. (2002). What we know about bias and intergroup conflict, the problem of the century. *Current Directions in Psychological Science, 11*(4), 123–128.

Hymel, S., Wagner, E., & Butler, L. (1990). Reputational bias: View from the peer group. In S. R. Ascher & J. Coie (Eds.), *Peer rejection in childhood* (pp. 156–186). Cambridge, England: Cambridge University Press.

Kohlberg, L. (1984). *Essays in moral development: Vol. 2. The psychology of moral development.* San Francisco: Harper & Row.

Mackie, D. M., Hamilton, D. L., Susskind, J., & Rosselli, F. (1996). Social psychological foundations of stereotype formation. In C. Macrae, C. Stangor, & M. Hewstone (Eds.), *Stereotypes and stereotyping* (pp. 41–77). New York: Guilford.

Neff, K. D., & Terry-Schmitt, L. N. (2002). Youths' attributions for power-related gender attributes: Nature, nurture, or God? *Cognitive Development, 17*(2), 1185–1202.

Opotow, S. (1990). Moral exclusion and injustice: An introduction. *Journal of Social Issues, 46,* 1–20.

Prencipe, A., & Helwig, C. C. (2002). The development of reasoning about the teaching of values in school and family contexts. *Child Development, 73,* 841–846.

Rosi, A. S. (1973). "Remember the ladies": Abigail Adams vs. John Adams. In A. S. Rosi (Ed.), *The feminist papers: From Adams to de Beauvoir* (pp. 7–15). New York: Bantam.

Smetana, J. G. (1995). Morality in context: Abstractions, ambiguities, and applications. In R. Vasta (Ed.), *Annals of Child Development* (Vol. 10, pp. 83–130). London: Jessica Kingsley.

Staub, E. (1987). *The roots of evil: The origins of genocide and other group violence.* Cambridge: England: Cambridge University Press.

Turiel, E. (1998). The development of morality. In W. Damon (Ed.), *Handbook of child psychology,* & N. Eisenberg, (Vol. Ed.), *Vol. 3. Socialization* (5th ed., pp. 863–932). New York: Wiley.

CONTRIBUTORS

Melanie Killen (PhD, 1985, University of California, Berkeley) is Professor of Human Development and Associate Director of the Center for Children, Relationships, and Culture at the University of Maryland. She is co-editor (with Daniel Hart) of *Morality in Everyday Life: Developmental Perspectives*, co-editor (with Jonas Langer) of *Piaget, Evolution, and Development*, and editor of *Children's Autonomy, Social Competence and Interactions with Adults and Children*. Her research area is social and moral development, including social reasoning about group inclusion and exclusion, implicit biases about groups, and cultural influences on development.

Jennie Lee-Kim (BA, 1994, Vanderbilt University) is a doctoral student at the University of Maryland. Her dissertation is on how Korean-American children evaluate parental expectations regarding boys' and girls' peer activity preferences.

Heidi McGlothlin (BA, Western Kentucky University) is a doctoral student at the University of Maryland. Her dissertation is on children's implicit racial biases and the role of social experience on these types of biases.

Charles Stangor (BA, Western Kentucky University) is Professor of Psychology at the University of Maryland. He is co-editor (with Neil Macrae and Miles Hewstone) of *Stereotypes and Stereotyping* and co-editor (with Janet Swim) of *Prejudice: The Target's Perspective*. His research area is intergroup relations, with a focus on stereotyping and prejudice.

Charles C. Helwig (Ph.D., 1991, University of California, Berkeley) is Associate Professor and Associate Chair of the Department of Psychology, University of Toronto. He is a Consulting Editor for *Child Development* and the *SRCD Monographs*. His general interests are in the areas of social cognition and moral development, with particular research interests in the development of reasoning about rights, democracy, and values.

STATEMENT OF EDITORIAL POLICY

The *Monographs* series is devoted to publishing developmental research that generates authoritative new findings and uses these to foster fresh, better integrated, or more coherent perspectives on major developmental issues, problems, and controversies. The significance of the work in extending developmental theory and contributing definitive empirical information in support of a major conceptual advance is the most critical editorial consideration. Along with advancing knowledge on specialized topics, the series aims to enhance cross-fertilization among developmental disciplines and developmental sub fields. Therefore, clarity of the links between the specific issues under study and questions relating to general developmental processes is important. These links, as well as the manuscript as a whole, must be as clear to the general reader as to the specialist. The selection of manuscripts for editorial consideration, and the shaping of manuscripts through reviews-and-revisions, are processes dedicated to actualizing these ideals as closely as possible.

Typically *Monographs* entail programmatic large-scale investigations; sets of programmatic interlocking studies; or—in some cases—smaller studies with highly definitive and theoretically significant empirical findings. Multi-authored sets of studies that center on the same underlying question can also be appropriate; a critical requirement here is that all studies address common issues, and that the contribution arising from the set as a whole be unique, substantial, and well integrated. The needs of integration preclude having individual chapters identified by individual authors. In general, irrespective of how it may be framed, any work that is judged to significantly extend developmental thinking will be taken under editorial consideration.

To be considered, submissions should meet the editorial goals of *Monographs* and should be no briefer than a minimum of 80 pages (including references and tables). There is an upper limit of 175–200 pages. In exceptional circumstances this upper limit may be modified (please submit four copies). Because a *Monograph* is inevitable lengthy and usually

131

substantively complex, it is particularly important that the text be well organized and written in clear, precise, and literate English. Note, however, that authors from non-English speaking countries should not be put off by this stricture. In accordance with the general aims of SRCD, this series is actively interested in promoting international exchange of developmental research. Neither membership in the Society nor affiliation with the academic discipline of psychology are relevant in considering a *Monographs* submission.

The corresponding author for any manuscript must, in the submission letter, warrant that all coauthors are in agreement with the content of the manuscript. The corresponding author also is responsible for informing all coauthors, in a timely manner, of manuscript submission, editorial decisions, reviews received, and any revisions recommended. Before publication, the corresponding author also must warrant in the submission letter that the study has been conducted according to the ethical guidelines of the Society for Research in Child Development.

Potential authors who may be unsure whether the manuscript they are planning would make an appropriate submission are invited to draft an outline of what they propose, and send it to the Editor for assessment. This mechanism, as well as a more detailed description of all editorial policies, evaluation processes, and format requirements can be found at the Editorial Office web site (http://astro.temple.edu/~overton/monosrcd.html) or by contacting the Editor, Willis F. Overton, Temple University-Psychology, 1701 North 13th St. – Rm 567, Philadelphia, PA 19122-6085 (e-mail: monosrcd@blue.temple.edu) (telephone: 1-215-204-7360).

Monographs of the Society for Research in Child Development (ISSN 0037-976X), one of three publications of the Society for Research in Child Development, is published four times a year by Blackwell Publishers, Inc., with offices at 350 Main Street, Malden, MA 02148, USA, and 108 Cowley Road, Oxford OX4 1JF, UK. Call US 1-800-835-6770, fax: (781) 388-8232, or e-mail: subscrip@ blackwellpub.com. A subscription to *Monographs of the SRCD* comes with a subscription to *Child Development* (published six times a year in February, April, June, August, October, and December). A combined package rate is also available with the third SRCD publication, *Child Development Abstracts and Bibliography*, published three times a year.

INFORMATION FOR SUBSCRIBERS For new orders, renewals, sample copy requests, claims, change of address, and all other subscription correspondence, please contact the Journals Subscription Department at the publisher's Malden office.

INSTITUTIONAL SUBSCRIPTION RATES FOR MONOGRAPHS OF THE SRCD/CHILD DEVELOPMENT 2002 The Americas $293, Rest of World £192. All orders must be paid by credit card, business check, or money order. Checks and money orders should be made payable to Blackwell Publishers. Canadian residents please add 7% GST.

INSTITUTIONAL SUBSCRIPTION RATES FOR MONOGRAPHS OF THE SRCD/CHILD DEVELOPMENT 2002 The Americas $328, Rest of World £232. All orders must be paid by credit card, business check, or money order. Checks and money orders should be made payable to Blackwell Publishers. Canadian residents please add 7% GST.

BACK ISSUES Back issues are available from the publisher's Malden office.

MICROFORM The journal is available on microfilm. For microfilm service, address inquiries to ProQuest Information and Learning, 300 North Zeeb Road, Ann Arbor, MI 48106-1346, USA. Bell and Howell Serials Customer Service Department: 1-800-521-0600 ×2873.

POSTMASTER Periodicals class postage paid at Boston, MA, and additional offices. Send address changes to Blackwell Publishers, 350 Main Street, Malden, MA 02148, USA.

CURRENT

Lightning Source UK Ltd.
Milton Keynes UK
15 October 2009

144994UK00001BA/3/P